DANIELLE BAYARD JACKSON

Give it a Rest

The Case for Tough-Love Friendships

Copyright © 2019 by Danielle Bayard Jackson

All rights reserved. No part of this publication may be reproduced, stored or transmitted in any form or by any means, electronic, mechanical, photocopying, recording, scanning, or otherwise without written permission from the publisher. It is illegal to copy this book, post it to a website, or distribute it by any other means without permission.

Danielle Bayard Jackson asserts the moral right to be identified as the author of this work.

Danielle Bayard Jackson has no responsibility for the persistence or accuracy of URLs for external or third-party Internet Websites referred to in this publication and does not guarantee that any content on such Websites is, or will remain, accurate or appropriate.

Designations used by companies to distinguish their products are often claimed as trademarks. All brand names and product names used in this book and on its cover are trade names, service marks, trademarks and registered trademarks of their respective owners. The publishers and the book are not associated with any product or vendor mentioned in this book. None of the companies referenced within the book have endorsed the book.

First edition

ISBN: 978-0-578-56756-3

This book was professionally typeset on Reedsy.
Find out more at reedsy.com

Contents

Preface	iv
The Problem All Around Us	1
The Four Sectors of Tough-Love Friendship	12
Intimacy in Friendship	20
You, Me, Us: The Benefits of Tough-Love Friendship	37
When Culture Holds Us Back	49
Sociology is a Mother	56
I Feel Your Pain (and Other Crazy Wiring)	64
When It's All in Your Head	74
Tough Love: How to Give It	82
Tough Love: How to Take It	99
When You're Wary of Her Choices	112
When Insecurities Get in the Way	120
Calling it Out: Gossip and Complaining	126
Holding Up Her Mirror	137
One-Sided Friendships and Spiritual Perspective	145
Discussion Questions	154
Acknowledgements	158
About the Author	159

Preface

I began writing this book at 2:30A.M. on a chilly morning in January 2019. It all started because a close friend said something to me that literally kept me up all night, her comments replaying in my mind as I tossed and turned in bed next to my (patient) husband. What began as a stream-of-conscious journal entry to purge racing thoughts quickly became an eight-month-long obsession.

I've spent the last ten years of my life speaking with women about honesty, communication, and friendship. I did this as a college student, a high school teacher, a publicist, and most recently as a women's coach. In every capacity of my history, I've found myself having conversations with other women about the nuances of female friendship, and from those talks I've come to one undeniable conclusion: *there's just so much that we aren't saying to each other.*

During this time, I never thought to write a book. I took each conversation for what it was, enjoying the insight I gathered from every woman who shared her story with me. But I noticed certain themes emerging, and there were unspoken fears I kept hearing which eventually compelled me to give voice to my observations.

I found the level of duality in female friendship to be completely bizarre. There's what we say and do and then there's what we *really* want to say and do. This is not, as one might carelessly conclude, because we're fake or calculating. Instead, I found that there's a whole host of powerful and invisible factors that influence the way we interact (and don't interact) with each other. And the only way we're going to conquer our anxieties, challenge the culture, and speak up for ourselves is to finally have *the conversation*.

Perhaps another reason I was driven to write *Give it a Rest* is because I used to be a "mean girl"— yeah, you know the type. But age and life experience matured and softened me. Dealing with 18-year-old's as a teacher really opened my eyes to the power of compassion; running my own business has shown me the importance of diplomacy; and becoming a mother has created in me a great tenderness— it's all worked to change my perspective on *toughness*. But as I've grown out of my old ways, there's one belief I still hold tight: *the idea of tough-love friendships.*

One thing I always notice among "nice girls" is the superficiality in some of their friendships as they cower from saying what they mean. While I've made several mistakes as a friend, I realize that giving (and receiving) tough-love with other women is the way to experience real freedom and depth in our friendships. And while I advocate for speaking up, I also learned that "telling it like it is" becomes ineffective (and even harmful) if it's not delivered with grace. I've discovered the way to say what you mean with both boldness and compassion— and I think what I've found just might save our friendships.

In a culture pushing us to be "nice" and in a time when the opportunity for meaningful connection seems more distant than ever before, there are a myriad of reasons why we're playing it safe in our relationships with other women.

But I'd like to make a case against that.

Here are some thoughts you'll likely have while reading:
1. Girl, YES! Preach!
2. Huh, I disagree with that.
3. Well, that's offensive.
4. Hmm, I've never considered that.

5. I've heard this before.
6. Well, that's dumb. I can't apply that.
7. This is brilliant. I can't wait to apply this.

And let's be real, as long as your responses to the book aren't only numbers 2, 5, and 6, I'm cool with that.

Your insecurities about speaking truthfully; your misconceptions about real friendship; your doubts about showing up: GIVE IT A REST and let's get to the heart of the matter.

As you read, whip out your highlighter and mark up the pages. I want you to really make this book your own, annotating the lines that speak to you and placing question marks in the areas where you disagree with what you've read. Use those particular points as conversation-starters when you go out with friends or pose them as questions to your followers on social media. The whole point is for us to engage in conversation that ultimately leads to more honest friendships.

For those of you reading this book with friends, you'll find discussion questions in the back. Feel free to answer them as you read or save them until the end. Either way, grab a glass of your favorite wine, a ballpoint pen, and get your best friend on the phone.

Then turn the page and join me as we explore ways to experience more realness in our friendships with a little thing called "tough love".

The Problem All Around Us

Even I have to admit it was a pitiful scene.

Kneeling in a dark closet and clutching my phone to my ear, I heaved as salty tears trickled down my ashy cheeks. Snot-filled sobs grew louder and wilder by the second as I cried into the darkness.

"I mean, I just don't get it... I did everything! *sob* I supported the whole photography thing, you know? I went to his shows... and, and we took that trip to Miami, remember? *sob* I just don't—why does he keep lying to me? It's like I'm not... enough..."

I was bellowing and rocking back and forth. It was *not* a good look.

My friend, Erica, listened on the other end. She stammered through my blubbering, searching for the words to console me.

"Danni, I don't know what to say. I'm... I'm so sorry. He's a jerk! It's all going to work out. I don't know how but—it's all gonna work out!"

Had it been the first time I was calling Erica with this problem, her response would have been reasonable enough. Your friend calls you crying about something awful her boyfriend did? You tell her he's a loser and that things will be okay. That's Friendship 101.

But it wasn't the first time. I'd made this call to Erica several times before.

You see, it was 2007 and I had just uncovered, for the hundredth time, another one of my boyfriend's deceptions. It was also the hundredth time that I'd cried to friends about it, wondering what I'd done (or failed to do) for him to keep lying. For some reason, my anger and disappointment was never targeted at him, but directed inward toward myself. Initially, I think I did blame him. But as he continued to screw up, I began to question myself somewhere along the way. I lamented my inability to be enough to keep him honest.

It was ridiculous. I know that now. But man, when you are in the thick of your mess it is near impossible to think clearly.

What I needed to hear was that I was contributing to my own mistreatment. What I needed to hear was that despite my strength I was choosing to be weak. What I needed to hear was that my desperation for male companionship had made me a freaking hot mess.

But that reality check never came.

A few years after college graduation, friends admitted to me that they'd thought I was being weak and passive during those years, and that my complaining about my boyfriend in all of our conversations had made me difficult to be around. When I *was* with my boyfriend, I'd ditched them to spend time with him. And when we broke up, I unintentionally hijacked conversations with my friends, finding ways to connect it back to my ex.

They never told me at the time because they didn't want to piss me off. They didn't want to lose me as a friend. They didn't want to offend me.

But that's not what I needed.

I needed them to keep it real—to tell me to get up from the floor and wipe my face. I needed them to tell me that his defects were completely unrelated to what I had to offer as a woman. I needed to be reminded of my worth and to hear that my desperation had so intensely warped my mind that I was sacrificing logic and dignity for the approval of a man.

This doesn't absolve me of the personal responsibility I needed to take to get myself together. But ultimately, I needed a dose of tough love— to be told that my obsession had become toxic and my whining unbearable.

THE PROBLEM

Whether it's telling our friends that we feel used, invisible, or misunderstood, there are truths we withhold. And if everyone's doing it, that means we're not experiencing the depth and authenticity in our friendships. My college friends— despite the vulnerability that we shared and the encouragement we gave to each other— were missing other elements in our friendship that would have allowed us to experience more fulfillment, not only in our relationship with each other, but our individual lives.

We're hungry to be our full selves in our friendships: share our true feelings, voice our concerns, hold our friends accountable, and operate freely with mutual transparency and respect.

How do we keep it real with our friends in every way without risking the friendship itself? How do we "tell it like it is" without being labeled "rude"? How do we communicate our boundaries without being dismissed as oversensitive?

I've been searching for the answer for years.

For ten years, I've observed women in nearly every capacity:

I spent almost seven years as a high school teacher, and during that time I watched 18-year-old girls struggle with the complexities of friendship. The tension was obvious when I watched them anxiously walk the hallways, congregate in the cafeteria, and confess secret insecurities in hushed whispers when we were alone after class was dismissed.

I've listened to the women who gather for book club meetings. Having participated in several over the years, I'm no longer surprised when the conversation shifts from discussing a novel's plot points to comparing the protagonist's struggles with their own. After a few glasses of wine, women begin to share the pain they've endured at the hands of another woman.

As a publicist, I've marveled at the way a one-on-one interview prep with a client can suddenly turn into a coaching session as she admit her lack of confidence traces back to something hurtful a friend said years ago, or how she can't focus on the company crisis at hand because she's dealing with personal conflicts with her female co-founder. I always try to remain professional, but I find that— because of our strong and feminine hearts— we often blur the lines between work life and personal life, no matter how we try to separate the two... because they are so inextricably linked sometimes.

As a women's coach, I've grown more attuned to women's complaints about the changing dynamics in their friend groups, unspoken frustrations with the women closest to them, and general feelings of isolation and misunderstanding.

In each of these situations— as the teacher, the friend, the publicist, and the coach— I end the conversation by asking the woman I'm speaking with if she's shared her "heart troubles" with the friend she's talking about.

She always answers one of three ways:

1. *"No, I can't..."*
2. *"I want to, but I don't even know how I'd start..."*
3. *"Yeah, but it didn't go well..."*

Regardless of these women's beliefs, ages, professions, and backgrounds, they shared the same struggle: trying to navigate the uniquely complex nuances of female friendship.

These were women who'd experienced rejection, frustration, and confusion in dealings with their friends. But when it came to expressing their issues directly with the ladies in their lives, they either refused to address them, felt completely unequipped to have the conversation, or were totally wrong in their approach to the conflict.

When many of us address tension within our friendships, we're either way too passive and avoidant, or we engage with a strength so fierce that it just makes things worse.

How do we find the balance?

THE SOLUTION

Based on our respective past experiences, we may have different ideas of what "tough love" looks like.

When you hear someone mention "tough love", what do you think of? Do you picture the girl who's loudly "telling it like it is" without regard for others' feelings? Is she dropping "truth bombs" on people without remorse, and when called out about it, does she respond with something like, "Hey, I'm just being honest"? You're not alone in associating the phrase with this image, but it's a distorted version of what tough love is supposed to be. This definition doesn't account for the level of compassion required to share hard truths with a friend; it doesn't leave room for the vulnerability required of both women sitting at the table; it doesn't consider the emotions and consequences of sensitive but rewarding conversations.

Instead of conjuring an image of the quintessential "mean girl," picture the friend who is unafraid to lay a gentle but firm hand on your shoulder when things get rough, whispering, "Girl, you can do better. *We* can do better."

This is a more accurate picture of what "tough love" looks like and how it feels. It is inviting and understanding. It is honest and direct.

Tough-love friendship chooses to do hard, uncomfortable things because it values the woman more than the friendship.

It says, "I love you so much that I'm willing to risk our friendship for the sake of your well being." Whether she pushes you away or questions your loyalty, you stand courageously, willing to demand that she be the best version of herself—and that you are granted the freedom to do the same. And that can't happen if women are keeping their true feelings inside.

A PICTURE OF TOUGH-LOVE

In a friendship, tough-love looks like:

Refusing to enable a friend by giving into her self-destructive habits, such as suggesting a shopping trip if you know she doesn't spend money wisely; taking her to bars even though you know she'll binge drink again and regret the next day.

Sharing a hard truth. Her habit of cancelling last-minute is a pain…Her boss is taking advantage of her kindness and work ethic… Tough love kindly and courageously confronts the things other friends are too nervous to say.

Refusing to 'polite laugh' when she makes racist jokes; self-deprecating comments about her appearance, intelligence, or abilities; or when she speaks ill of other women.

Reminding her of her worth even though it may be difficult for her to accept praise and affirmation.

Boldly communicating your own needs, desires, boundaries, and expectations.

We need to find a way to boldly address the issues in our friendships. And we need to do it with directness, urgency, and compassion.

As I watched this theme emerge over the past decade, I went searching for resources to understand:

1. Why it's so difficult to say what we really want to say to our friends

2. The cultural pressures that influence our aversion to hard truths

3. What are the qualities, attitudes, and behaviors that help us to deepen our relationships with other women

4. How our independent and collective well being is directly affected by a willingness to be vulnerable in our relationships with other women

I couldn't find anything.

After questioning other women, I learned that the topic of unspoken conflict in female friendships is largely unexplored.

TECHNOLOGY MAKES IT HARDER

The definition of *friend* has expanded to include our co-workers, customers, classmates, and neighbors. With the prevalence of social media and one-click "friending," we now consider active Instagram followers whom we've never met to be our friends. While Instagram, Twitter, and Facebook, have made it possible to interact with women across the world, it's done little to help us form meaningful relationships with the capacity to withstand hardship, trials, and inconveniences. And it's all the more reason we are out of practice when it comes to having hard conversations— we have tons of "friendships" that don't require this difficult work.

Technology has also affected our willingness to show each other tough love. We have grown accustomed to tolerating what makes us uncomfortable in our friendships and we do it to maintain an appearance of harmony, so long as we still look like friends online (uploaded pictures of us arm-in-arm as #FRIENDSHIPGOALS dances along the caption line).

GIVE IT A REST

While our conditioned politeness and chronic avoidance may keep our follower count high, it does little for creating edifying friendships that challenge and fulfill us.

And isn't that one of the most fundamental goals of any friendship?

A truly deep relationship with another woman will bring with it inconveniences and messy complications. It's uncomfortable because we share ourselves, and in sharing ourselves, we invite someone to come along on the journey with us. But she joins us as more than a spectator, some passive passenger. No. She's an *active* participant in the process as we figure things out. She helps us to get on the right track— and that kind of support and accountability only comes with tough love and a willingness to tell the truth.

WHY WE NEED TOUGH-LOVE FRIENDSHIPS

While this kind of friendship helps others to be their best selves, it also helps the woman choosing to *give* tough love. Too often, we passively accept conditions and situations that materialize in our friendships despite the fact that they make us uncomfortable. And there are so many reasons we choose to keep our discomfort to ourselves, but no matter the reason, it's a habit we've gotta break. We suffer when we try to contain our frustrations and concerns, but in an effort to keep the peace, we hold it in anyway.

The irony here is this: While we are theoretically more comfortable with the people we call "friends," it's sometimes more difficult to address the hard stuff with them than with people we don't know. Perhaps it's because there's more at stake. Perhaps it's because after we share our truths, we have to see them again the next day. It's complicated, and it can threaten to disrupt the ecosystem of our relationship.

We instead choose to run away, both physically and emotionally.

But what if there was greater joy, self-assurance, intimacy, and understanding on the other side of a tough conversation?

An unpopular piece of advice that I give to help coaching clients looking to move toward a better life is to **boldly chase the hard things.** So much of what's holding us back in our lives is our refusal to communicate with the people around us.

Despite our closeness, we are afraid to communicate our true desires, needs, and boundaries.

In an effort to not rock the boat or to avoid confrontation, we withhold these truths, but we are in turn, being held hostage by our fears. If we don't find the courage to tell the people in our lives what we will and won't tolerate, we become complicit in our own misery.

Tough love means being strong for yourself, for your friends, and for your friendships. Whether that means voicing new boundaries or helping to keep her accountable, it requires a level of courage and compassion that can deepen the intimacy, connection, health, and overall REALNESS in your female relationships.

Politeness may keep the peace for a time. Avoidance may delay discomfort. But confronting our friends with what's challenging is a high calling— one that is required of all those in search of more meaningful friendships.

YOUR PERSONALITY IS WELCOME

Let me make this clear: It doesn't matter what your personality is, tough love is for you. So often women will dismiss confrontation as something that's just not in their personality, but doing the "hard things" is a requirement of us all. You may be an easygoing, bohemian wildflower, but inviting a friend to a difficult conversation is not a behavior contradictory to your personality type. In fact, for a more authentic conversation, your personality should be a part of your approach.

If you're an extroverted Type-A, there is room for your personality and style as well. Delivering tough-love truth-telling is something that only works if you're yourself, but while acting with certain considerations in mind.

I personally tend to add a bit of playfulness to situations that are serious or especially sensitive. This is not to minimize them with humor, but I work to find a way to gracefully add a lightness at points to help clear the tension. That's simply a part of my personality, and I can bring that part of myself to a tough love conversation.

Simply put: You shouldn't have to reach for a *persona* to do something difficult. In the following chapters you'll learn frameworks and guidelines to make it less difficult. There won't be any line-by-line scripts, though, because a genuine tough-love conversation is designed according to your unique strengths, needs, and personality. And you must show up to do it as yourself, not as a woman who's memorized her lines. Wearing a mask or pretending to be someone else to get you through a tough task can be a helpful tactic for some people in certain situations, but I'd like to think that showing up as yourself really develops a boldness, a confidence inside of you— and the experience itself is that much more rewarding.

You can actually do that very hard thing as the real you— you don't have to be in character. You can use all of your strengths and personal flair to help you be the best "tough love friend" you can be.

If you're the passive type, please know that you have the courage to confront hard things boldly. If you're the aggressive type, please know that you have the patience and capacity to confront hard things gently.

ANSWERS FOR THE QUESTIONS YOU CAN'T ASK

There are several reasons why we aren't having the conversation about being a "tough-love friend," which requires doing hard things for the sake of the friendship. I'll explore some of those reasons in the upcoming chapters, and I hope it will shed some light on why we do what we do and, more importantly, how we can change the trajectory of our friendships with "tough-love."

But, for now, just know that you are in the right place if you are:

A. relatively passive, trying to gather the courage to have a tough conversation with a friend,

B. often told that you can be too harsh, and you want to be a "tough love" friend in the right way,

C. looking for a friendship model to help you determine what's missing in your relationships with other women,

D. want to understand how to communicate better with the women in your life,

E. and are as curious as I am about the unspoken things that make women's friendships so special.

If the ultimate goal is to better our friends, our friendships, and ourselves, we've got to get it right. There's too much love and connection at stake.

Intimacy, strength, and joy are on the other side of *hard things*.

So, we'd better get to work.

The Four Sectors of Tough-Love Friendship

Before we can look at how to achieve and benefit from tough-love friendships, we have to first examine what it looks like. Then we have to honestly evaluate our own capacity to initiate and sustain this kind of friendship with the women in our lives (and those we haven't yet met!).

I've created what's called the "Tough-Love Friendship Model" and it's made up of four sectors. Use this as a guide when you are 1. trying to determine if a new friendship is worth it; 2. assessing what's missing from your current female relationships; and 3. looking for language to describe the complexities and nuance of the conflict you may be experiencing.

Let's jump right in.

THE FOUR COURAGE SECTORS OF THE TOUGH-LOVE FRIENDSHIP MODEL

A tough-love friendship has four important parts: *Sharing, Preserving, Affirming, and Challenging*. These are verbs that describe the action required in each of the four critical spaces. The most fulfilling and authentic friendships have both people operating in all areas.

Each sector also has an energy which I've labeled either "masculine" or "feminine." I can't stress enough that this has nothing to do with actual males or females, but instead, it simply refers to the *energy* carried in each sector. I believe anything holistic must include both types of energy to be effective.

THE FOUR SECTORS OF TOUGH-LOVE FRIENDSHIP

Let's take a look at each one, and as we do, consider your experience with them. Use the diagram for reference as we define each sector.

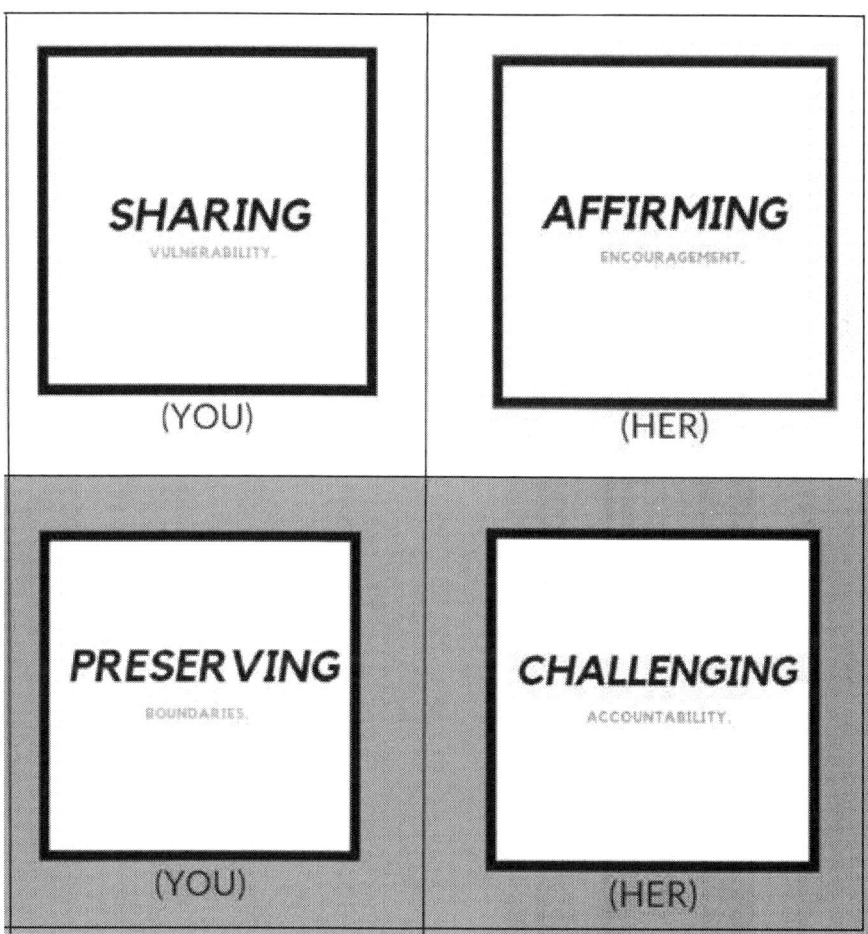

An image of The Tough-Love Friendship Model

The Tough-Love Friendship Model has four sectors.

The first two sectors are what tough love demands you do for <u>yourself</u>.

The first sector is *Sharing*.

This means that you must demonstrate vulnerability by sharing your personal feelings, secret desires, private fears and dreams, and failures and success. Faith is required here, as vulnerability often puts us in a space of risk, trusting the other woman not to reject or betray us when we reveal the most fragile parts of ourselves.

Some women navigate this sector with ease, as sharing their personal thoughts and feelings is cathartic and brings them closer to other women. But there are women who struggle with letting their guard down in this way. By now, many of us know the power and importance of being vulnerable, but we experience mental resistance when we try to put it in into practice, and that's normal. The key is to remember that friendships will stagnate and remain surface-level if you work to share only the safe and impersonal parts of yourself.

We have to exercise this with discretion and wisdom of course, doing it with the right people once they've shown some level of interest and trust, and have demonstrated the capacity to empathize and support us through the journey.

I also want to note that vulnerability is not just sharing your fears— it's having the courage to share *any* emotion. This could look like having the courage to share a success or win that you're having in a group full of women, something that it is very difficult to do because we risk looking "full of ourselves". But you be vulnerable enough to *celebrate* in front of your friends?

This Sharing sector requires that you must give of yourself openly and honestly to be known— to be truly seen.

You will not experience fulfillment from your friendships if you do not bring your most vulnerable parts to the table.

I've assigned a feminine energy to this sector because sharing feelings is a stereo-typically feminine attribute, although it is necessary for friendships of any gender. Verbal expression and emotional conversation are typically associated with females.

The consequence of a friendship without the *Sharing* sector is a lack of depth. A friendship without your full presence limits the depth and potential of your relationships with other women, only giving room for superficial interaction.

The second sector is *Preserving*.

You must not lose yourself in an attempt to maintain your friendship with another woman. If ever you begin to mute or dilute parts of yourself for the sake of another's comfort, you've done a great disservice to the relationship overall. The *Preserving* sector is all about boundaries and the freedom of personal expression. It requires you to exercise self-care within the relationship, with the freedom to express opinions that may be unpopular. It's in this sector that you show integrity for what you believe in, without fear of judgment or abandonment.

The *Preserving* sector asks that you be accountable to *yourself* by not only creating boundaries, but by keeping them. Self-preservation requires you to be mindful of your limitations, questioning the messages you receive, the environment you are in, and the things that you feel comfortable with. You must have the courage to put up guardrails that protect you (not out of fear, hardness, or defensiveness; rather, out of self-love) while you simultaneously engage in a healthy way with your friends.

While friendship is a beautiful space to create a bond and connection with someone, you must still be responsible for your emotional health and well being. The most intimate friendships allow you the space and autonomy to do just that.

From the wrong people, you may experience manipulative and immature responses to setting boundaries. They may tell you that you think you're "too good" for them or that "you're so different now". Prepare yourself to be met with misunderstanding and insecurity from some women who feel angered or threatened by you speaking up for your needs, and instead, look for those who welcome it. Look for the ones who see your boundaries as a helpful way to know how to respect you and properly navigate a friendship with you.

This *Preserving* sector also involves being able to receive hard truths from friends that help hold you accountable. It requires not only courage to erect boundaries, but humility to allow friends to help you uphold them when you begin to waver. That could come in the form of a "call-out." It could come in the form of affirmation. But there are things that both you and your friends must do to keep you physically, mentally, and emotionally safe.

The *Preserving* sector carries a masculine energy because firmly stating boundaries and voicing unpopular opinions is a trait stereotypically associated with men. This likely stems from the cultural expectation for females to be polite and agreeable while resistance is viewed as uniquely assertive on a man. Again, preservation is necessary in any real friendship— it just carries masculine energy. And tough-love demands both male and female energy.

The consequence of not operating in the *Preserving* sector is losing yourself. If you do not stand up for your beliefs, needs and boundaries, then it is likely because you are acquiescing to the beliefs, needs and boundaries of others, which is where you'll lose the foothold on your integrity. Without the courage to *Preserving*, one friend will gradually lose her independence and sense of self within the unit.

While the first two sector outline what you do for yourself in a tough-love friendship, sectors three and four describe what you are required to do for *others*.

***Affirming* is the third sector of The Tough-Love Friendship Model.**

This sector demands a joyful and relentless support for the other woman. It requires you to speak life into her during times of doubt, and to remind her of her worth when she questions her abilities and her place in this world. For the seasons she wonders if she's enough, you are the external force that whispers back to her, "Yes, girl! You are more than enough." The *Affirming* sector is where you help rediscover and reactivate her confidence as a woman to her inner self.

This sector calls for you to be her cheerleader, to be a good listener, and to be a champion of all she is and could be. **Where the *Sharing* sector is all**

THE FOUR SECTORS OF TOUGH-LOVE FRIENDSHIP

about *you* being seen, the *Affirming* sector is about seeing *her*.

Affirming has a feminine energy because openly and wildly encouraging someone is often seen as a female trait. As literal life-givers, we have an inclination to give life through our words, and while all friendships require mutual support, the very expressiveness of this quality points to a more feminine energy.

The consequence of a weak *Affirming* sector is selfishness. If a woman tends to every other area but is weak in the area of affirming, the friendship becomes one-sided as she (intentionally or unintentionally) uses it for her own advancement, emotional release, and support. Withholding affirmation for others in your relationships either comes from a place of insecurity, jealousy, or selfishness— regardless of the reason, it is a self-centered attitude that will get in the way of a healthy, mutually beneficial relationship. Tough-love friendship requires equal sharing, giving and support, but without a healthy *Affirming* sector, the other sectors' capacities are limited.

The final sector is about *Challenging*.

The *Challenging* sector holds friends accountable, lovingly calls out their missteps, and invites them to hard conversations. This sector makes room for divergence, and maintains emotional connection despite miscommunication, misunderstandings, and offenses. It demonstrates courage by reminding a woman of her own integrity and growth by holding up a mirror when things get tough.

Where the *Preserving* sector is for you to hold your own self accountable, the *Challenging* sector is for you to hold your <u>friend</u> accountable.

Some women are reluctant to explore this sector in their friendships because the word "challenge" makes them think of being rude and combative. But you have to strip this word of the negative associations in order to experience the beauty in it. Try to remember that the word means to invite someone to engage. It is an opportunity for reflection and refinement. When you see a challenge as an opportunity instead of an obstacle, it will completely transform not only your friendships, but all of your relationships.

As we travel through life, we continually adapt and re-calibrate. We make vows to ourselves, and we are constantly refining our values and commitments. Naturally, we falter on these commitments, but we are more likely to maintain them when we have someone in our lives who reminds us of the responsibility. In fact, we're 65% likely to meet a goal if they shared it with another person. But that number increases to 95% if they're having ongoing meetings with that person (The American Society of Training and Development). While "tough-love friendship" is not formal arrangement, it is very much an arrangement with a built-in accountability buddy for life. But if the friend we select to fulfill this role only gives us empty platitudes and is too passive to help us address hard truths, this aspect of the friendship isn't activated.

Because of the way "call-outs" are stereotypically associated with male behavior, this sector is assigned a *masculine* energy. But again, the Tough-Love Friendship Model thrives because it's a holistic approach to achieving fulfilling relationships, and any holistic model is made of both male and female energy.

The consequence of not operating in the *Challenging* sector of the Tough-Love Friendship Model is imbalance. If you are allowing your friend to show up for you while you are not doing the same for her, then she loses and you are refusing to tap into your authority and accountability partner as her confidante. Refusing to navigate this sector does a disservice to the other woman, who expects to receive enrichment and growth from an open and honest friendship with you.

FOUR SECTORS IN HARMONY

The byproduct of a healthy *Sharing, Preserving, Affirming,* and *Challenging* sector is INTIMACY.

When each woman is sharing her feelings in a safe space; holding tightly to her identity, integrity and beliefs; showing caring and support for one another; and growing in a space that brings accountability and differing ideas, a rich and authentic friendship has room to develop. This is the kind of relationship that allows each woman to experience a close and fulfilling bond while also maintaining her "oneness".

Ultimately, it's the kind of friendship we're all hungry for.

Intimacy in Friendship

Intimacy is present when both women can bring their full selves—their beliefs, limitations, weaknesses, insecurities and opinions—to the friendship and express themselves without fear of abandonment or judgment. And when those differences emerge and inevitably, cause tension and disagreement however, true intimacy knows how to recover.

INTIMACY V. CLOSENESS

The main issue I see with this word is its misuse: *Intimacy* is so often used synonymously with the word "closeness." While both words may stir up the same warm and snuggly feelings, they're wildly different.

Intimacy is a space where two people have exposed their true selves and still maintain an emotional connection in spite of diverging ideas and opinions. There is conflict and disagreement, along with familiarity, selflessness and growth. Over time, our capacity for intimacy is tested.

Intimacy keeps the connection even during the seasons when it doesn't feel exciting and fun.

Closeness, however, refers more to a *feeling*. It is the emotion associated with having affection for someone we've come to know. Closeness can be established in the first meeting—if the conversation is personal, humor is in sync, and eye contact is strong, it can leave two women feeling a connection; a chemistry. But it's not until time has passed, when they've shared their respective cultures, expressed different beliefs, and challenged each other, that true intimacy is developed.

We love the "girl-power" memes on social media: "If you can't love all of me, then you don't deserve me,"(cue likes, double-taps, "hell yeah's" in the comment section). While we *search* for acceptance, patience, and understanding in our friendships, we must ask ourselves if we're also able to *give* that same unconditional, non-judgmental space to others. Intimacy thrives in a relationship with mutual acceptance and vulnerability.

Women are complex, multi-dimensional beings, and though many of us acknowledge this intellectually, we don't always honor it in practice. Are we willing to make room for others' "otherness"?

Intimacy is formed when you can remain friends in spite of your differences. I'm not just referring to another woman's flaws and vices. I'm talking about accepting the parts of another woman that you don't understand. The parts that are different from what you grew up knowing… the parts of her that operate under a culture that is different from your own.

And once intimacy is achieved, it can also be irreparably damaged by a breach of trust, or a revelation that you simply can't recover from.

This point was made incredibly clear through a conversation I had with a woman at an event in St. Petersburg, Florida.

THE EXTENT OF INTIMACY

Hillary Van Dyke is the Senior Professional Development Coordinator for

Equity in for schools in Pinellas County, Florida. Her current work with racial equity and awareness was sparked by experiences she had as a young Black girl in a predominately white area. One particular situation came to mind when I questioned her about her experience with female friendship.

She told me about a platonic relationship with a white woman she grew up with and how close they'd become during their time together. The two attended college together and were practically inseparable.

One night, they began getting ready for a party in true, excitable college-girl fashion. They chatted eagerly on the way to the party and were looking forward to all the night had in store. But as they began walking toward the house that was hosting the event, she noticed her friend's quick pace slowed to a cautious slow-step.

"What's the matter?" Hillary asked, puzzled.

Her friend answered cautiously: "It's just— I just don't want to go inside."

Confused by the sudden change of heart, Hillary asked, "Why not?"

"Everybody's black. I don't want to stay here."

Her friend spat the words out, unequivocally disgusted... or nervous... or both. She showed surprise and impatience for Hillary's shock as she completely reeled from the comment.

Hillary was stunned. And it was in that moment when she realized that despite all their inside jokes and shared experiences, they would never be as close. Her friend not only saw the world with a perverted sense of racial superiority, but Hillary— completely unaware before this moment of her friend's worldview— would no longer experience intimate friendship with her because of it.

"I went to all-white parties with her all the time. I was always the minority. And the one time she was the minority she couldn't do it. I never called her out for saying that. I was too surprised at the time to say anything right away. But something definitely changed between us."

Regardless of race, friendship itself is about being able to bring all of yourself to the relationship. In cross-racial friendships, some women of color admit to not feeling a complete sense of intimacy with their white friends because they can't show up 100% as they are.

Hillary explained that for minorities, race is an inextricable thread in the fabric of who they are. And if friendship is ultimately about bringing your whole self to the table, then white friends who either ignore, tokenize, or separate one's race from his or her identity... well, can they really say they're able to show up for their friend?

Hillary lays plain the difficulty with and importance of acceptance of those who are different: "If you want to be my friend, then you have to realize that part of my identity is as a Black woman."

Healthy Digression

To my brown girls, I want to validate you right now: No, you are not crazy to feel a subtle, unspoken separation when you suffer micro-aggressions at hands of white women who are your friends. Most times, these comments and behaviors are well-intentioned. It's just that navigating a friendship where you have to explain yourself (your heritage and culture), absorb harmless offenses, or tiptoe around expressing your pain when another innocent black man is shot by police... it's exhausting. And simply put, you tire of withholding parts of yourself for sake of peace in the friendship. I get that. I see you. I've been there. I just want to affirm your thoughts when you recognize that sometimes with some non-POC you feel a lack of intimacy—it's not in your head. And at the risk of oversimplifying a very complex and historical issue, I'll just say that it's because your whole self, culture included, is not wholly accepted or invited to the friendship.

To my white friends, I challenge you to be aware of the times a friend of color must mute, explain, dilute, or defend her cultural practices, pain, or beliefs. Are you resistant? Do you tell her that perhaps the discrimination she's facing is imagined? Do you change the topic or get fired up when she voices parts of herself that make you uncomfortable? I have no nine-step program or tips on how to reconcile this, I just encourage you to evaluate your cross-racial friendships and see how accepting (not just tolerant, but inviting) you are of her world, and how it may impact your ability to be as close as you could be.

Just sayin'.

Hillary's experience set the foundation for how she now meaningfully engages in conversations at the intersection of race and friendship. During our interview, I asked her about how she'd advise women on addressing a tough conversation about race with a friend:

When it comes to having hard conversations about race, I approach my white friends the way I would anyone else: with honesty and directness. And it's a matter of energy output. I ask, "Do I care enough about this person or issue to use the energy it takes to address this?" If the issue is specifically about saying or doing something racist, that can be a moral issue. I try not to tell anyone how to live, but if it's a question of humanity I have to call it out. Why? Because that's where hate crimes emerge. And if you don't have the courage to call that out, then at the very least don't be around it.

Think about the relationships you've have with a few women in your life: Can they talk about things that make you uncomfortable? Can they bring you heartache that you don't understand? Can you still be friends when you discover they voted for the very policy that gets your blood boiling?

Let me be clear: I'm certainly not suggesting you accept everything and anything from another woman for the sake of starting a friendship. It's the things we have in common that connect us, after all. I'm just waving a huge, block-letter banner that says true intimacy does not look like chemistry and sameness. It looks like emotional connection that makes room for (and sometimes even thrives on) divergence.

While Hillary specifically addresses issues about race in the context of friendship, the general matter of intimacy appears here. A woman must take inventory of her friendships, examining the issues that are standing in the way of her bringing her complete self to the relationship. What it your capacity to present and accept a woman who thinks, behaves or appears differently?

When you think of differences, consider more than culture and interests.

Also consider the way we cope with stress and deal with tension. Perhaps you and a friend share several interests and have great communication. It's likely that bond will be tested when you experience tension together as a unit.

CONNECTION IN THE MIDST OF DIFFERENCES

At a recent GIVE IT A REST Movement Coaching event, women gathered to talk about their experiences with female friendship. We covered many topics that evening, and one that drew a lot of commentary was the subject of conflict.

A 20-year-old girl shared that she has many friends who misunderstand her when she asks for space to figure things out on her own.

"They're so quick to want to help give me advice and help me fix things, but I don't need that. I prefer to do it by myself."

She faces conflict as each person tries to show up for her according to their personal personalities and preferences. The challenge is in showing up for a friend in the way that fits her needs and respects her boundaries (operating in the *Challenging* sector of the Friendship model as she exercises her strength in the *Preserving* sector).

A 32-year-old woman sitting beside the young woman responded, "Well, I'm an independent thinker, too, but when things get really hard, I want my friends' help, I just don't wanna have to say it. They should know and come ready to help me figure it out without me having to say— if we know each other well, then they'll just know."

A college student listening intently to their exchange shared her stress management style: "I've had other girls push me to open up and I'll tell them, if it's something really difficult, 'I can't talk about that with you.' I don't feel bad about it either."

I offered a thought for her to consider, "And in a time when we are encouraging women to be more vulnerable and open, those girls probably see your refusal to share as a sign you don't trust them or that you're not as invested in the friendship."

"Exactly. They're insulted by it. But for me, that's just my boundary. I may not want to relive it. But that doesn't mean I am pushing away. I still want to be close to them. Those are just my boundaries... I've lost friends over that."

Remember, intimacy is the ability to maintain an emotional connection while your diverging attitudes, conflict styles and personalities remain dissimilar. If your friend prefers to work out her issues without external guidance, would it turn you off? If you had a friend who sought your insight at every turn, would it overwhelm you or would you take it as a flattering sign of her trust and affection?

If you had a passive friend who went out of her way to avoid conflict, would you feel like you weren't getting the chance to know the real her? Would her avoidance and withdrawal make it difficult for you to feel close to her? If you had a friend who was competitive during the times you found it unnecessary, would it eventually become more than you can handle? Or would your friendship make room for her competitive spirit?

A PICTURE OF HARMONY

Harriet Goldhor Lerner is a clinical psychologist and the author of several books including The Dance of Intimacy. In it she explores the effects of relationships between people with different conflict styles:

> *If our style of managing a stressful event is to share feelings and seek greater togetherness, we may rail against that other person whose preferred mode of handling the same stress is to be more private and self-reliant. If we tend to shift into an over-responsible, "fix-it" mode when anxiety hits, we may get all ruffled about that other person who reacts to stress with under-responsiveness... And the more intensely we do our thing, the more they do theirs... And the more we get stuck on the other person's behavior rather than our own, the more stuck we become.*

This may be where you begin thinking, "Well, I can't accept everything. I have preferences in the kinds of people I get close to— so I can't have intimacy with everyone."

You're absolutely right.

Intimacy is so special because it's rare and takes time to develop, so naturally it's impossible to experience with tons of people. That's what makes it so treasured. That's why it's so exceptional when two people finally arrive to that place.

Yet in light of this reality, I encourage you to evaluate whether there are friends in your life currently with whom you could experience a deeper connection if you were more open to sticking around once these differences emerged, putting in the effort to figure out how to navigate a friendship when these kinds of divergences are present.

I truly believe that one reason we are not experiencing more fullness in our female friendships is because we abandon them before they have a chance to grow. Based on the interactions I've observed over the years, women feel such strong connection fairly quickly… and intensely (due to our capacity for empathy, or connection through conversation and shared experiences, and our deep reading of subtext and nonverbal cues). A strong *feeling* of closeness grows and the "chemistry" overtakes us. Closeness is so nice to have, and it's the starting point of most friendships. When we form a closeness with another woman, we are suddenly seen—we are known. There's a gesture, a joke, a confession, and then it's all over. We like each other. It's instant. It's magical.

PUSHING PAST CONFLICT

But here is why so many of us mess up…

When the chemistry we feel with another woman is thwarted by an offensive comment, an unsavory habit or behavior, or any other discrepancy or "off-ness", we begin to wonder. If she falls off with the calls and texts, we don't pursue her for fear of rejection— or worse, we create a narrative in our minds of what her reason is for disappearing and write her off. Completely disenchanted, we question everything we thought we knew. Then we end it. And we replace her.

Largely preached in the context of romantic relationships, the idea of "staying once the magic's gone" is not foreign to us. We know that to build something long-lasting with a partner, we have to accept them, flaws and all.

In every other area of our lives, we know conflict is inevitable. But when it comes to friendship, we abandon this concept, holding fast to the expectation that it should be easy to begin and fun to sustain.

But it's just not true. In fact, research shows that women who believe friendship is "organic" are more likely to experience loneliness five years later, as opposed to women who acknowledge that friendship requires work.

LEVELS OF INTIMACY in FRIENDSHIP

There are varying levels of intimacy.

The <u>first level of intimacy</u>, as I've observed it, is **"safe talk."** This involves pleasant exchanges that are relatively harmless and don't require much emotional investment. You remain guarded, and share easy things about yourself, while each person gets a feel for the other's personality in a non-threatening space.

The <u>second level of intimacy</u> is **personal expression**. This level involves revealing more of your personal thoughts and opinions. You may also open up about past experiences, giving the other person insight into your world. There is some emotional investment at this level.

The <u>highest level of intimacy</u> in friendship involves **"diverging personhood."** This is where each person can bring herself (and the fullness of her SHARING and PRESERVING courage sectors) to the friendship and still enjoy acceptance from and connection with her friends. She can maintain her independent spirit while also being loyal to the unit. If there is vulnerability, boundaries, encouragement, and accountability in a friendship over time, this is how intimacy emerges.

TYPES OF INTIMACY in FRIENDSHIP

When I hear women talk about how they crave more intimacy in their friendships, they'll typically describe what they're looking for by outlining what they expect to *receive*: "I want the kind of friend I can share everything with… I want to be my total self… I'd love a girlfriend who has my back…"

But the key to developing intimacy (and closeness) in a friendship is defined not only by what you need from others, but also by what's required of you.

Here are the different types of intimacy along with reflection questions to determine your capacity to give and receive within each type:

Emotional: This type of intimacy considers each woman's feelings.

Your needs: Are you able to openly express how you feel, without reservation?

Her needs: Can you listen to another woman share her fears, joys, and frustrations and support her without judgment or discomfort?

Spiritual: This type of intimacy involves exchanging ideas and emotions surrounding an existential realm.

Your needs: Are you open to asking questions and sharing beliefs with another woman?

Her needs: Will you join your friend in conversation or experiences concerning spirituality, or is it something you prefer to explore independently of your friendships?

Intellectual: This type of intimacy involves sharing ideas that are cerebral—perhaps philosophy, academia, analyses of current events.

Your needs: Can you dissect intellectual ideas with another woman freely? Does she challenge and advance your understanding of the world in a way that feels helpful, not combative or belittling?

Her needs: Are you willing to join another woman in deep conversation? Can you listen and entertain her high-level ideas, or do you typically prefer conversation that is light and fun?

Experiential: This type of intimacy involves engaging in activities together and sharing experiences.

Your needs: Does your friend make time to do things with you, or does she prefer to text? When you hangout together, does it feel like she is fully present?

Her needs: Are you willing to spend time with your friend, or do you prefer phone calls? Does your schedule allow for pockets of quality time that you can give to your friends, or are you "too busy"?

TOUGH LOVE and INTIMACY

How close should you be before you begin exercising tough love principles? You do not have to be close or know each other for a certain period of time before you begin navigating he four courage sectors of the Tough-Love Friendship Model.

Sometimes you'll find that you easily fall into some sectors and have to work at the others. Perhaps it's easy for you to challenge your friend and keep her accountable, but it's more difficult for you to open up and share about your past experiences. Perhaps it's second nature for you to encourage your friend with kind words, but it's hard for you to speak those words to yourself when it's time to stand strong on issues you feel strongly about.

Remember that meaningful friendship takes time to develop, so be patient with your friends… and be patient with yourself. Try to recover when there's a misunderstanding. Communicate your concerns when they come up. Take a moment to process when you don't know how to react to something. Be slow to judge. Don't take offense when your girlfriends push for your actions to match your words.

WHEN YOUR ATTACHMENT STYLE IMPACTS YOUR FRIENDSHIP

Psychology addresses four types of attachment styles, and whenever someone is speaking on attachment styles, it's in the context of a parent-child relationship (which makes sense, as that's where our attachment style is first developed) and a romantic relationship. Interestingly, there's less application to platonic friendships.

Let me outline (very fundamentally) each kind of attachment style along with how it can impact your capacity for intimacy with your girlfriends:

SECURE ATTACHMENT: These people tend to have what's known as "emotional intelligence" and can gauge when their friends need space— and they're not threatened by it. Those with secure attachments are able to enjoy time together while also appreciating "alone time." They feel comfortable with being honest and have high levels of self-awareness. Though they enjoy support that comes along with companionship, they do not need it to feel secure or loved.

Friendships with this kind of woman will give you the freedom to be busy; it doesn't take cancelled plans personally, it allows you to have diverging beliefs and opinions and sticks around anyway. This kind of relationship is not threatened by you making other friends. It will affirm and support you, and communicate needs and desires without a fear of being judged, abandoned, or misunderstood.

ANXIOUS-PREOCCUPIED: These people are overly concerned with being important and considered by their friends. Their bonds tend to be intense as they enter friendships where one may serve as "savior" to the other, rescuing her from drama or self-inflicted trouble. There are mood swings often dictated by how the friendships feels that day, taking a day-by-day approach to the relationship instead of a rational and holistic aerial view. These women are often disappointed easily in their relationships with other women because they have a romanticized perspective of friendship. Low self-esteem is certainly at work here.

Friendships with this kind of woman may leave the girls in her life feeling like they have high expectations to live up to, and they unintentionally disappoint her often. This woman is threatened by her friends making new friends, and she needs her thoughts and feelings validated constantly. For the ANXIOUS-PREOCCUPIED woman, having a friend who will rescue her from self-destructive behavior is important— she may also have the opposite need, seeking friends who she can save.

DISMISSIVE-AVOIDANT: This attachment style describes a woman who is perceived as "Ms. Independent." While she wants meaningful relationships like anyone else, she remains emotionally distant. She'll keep her guard up and can be heard boasting about her ability to "cut-off" anyone who crosses her. She doesn't have many close relationships, and in the few she does have, she spends a lot of alone time and maintains her distance.

Friendships with this kind of woman can feel lonely or one-sided. You may find you're the one initiating hang-outs, and you may feel like she's not giving the same level of emotional vulnerability as you do. Although she does value your friendship, you may perceive her independence as a lack of care or emotional investment. She cares but may isolate herself as a defensive mechanism against possible pain and disappointment.

FEARFUL-AVOIDANT: This kind of attachment feels unpredictable in a relationship. There can be times they are clingy out of hunger for closeness, but there can just as easily be distance for fear of getting hurt. This person may even go as far as to hurt another friend out of fear of the intensity of their closeness. Because of the "hot-and-cold" nature of the friendship, this person is not close to many people.

Friendship with a woman of this attachment style is unpredictable. It can be frustrating as she struggles to be consistent about what she wants, and being involved with her can be hurtful as you're subjected to her whims and mercurial attitude.

WHEN INTIMACY DOESN'T LAST

One thing that would save us a lot of stress and frustration would be to accept that you *will* have friends who are close to you now but won't be later. It's inevitable. Why is that? Because life takes us through so many different stages and as we independently grow and change, it's only natural that those independent changes will either bring us closer together, shift us to new spaces, or completely separate us.

For some, our relationships change because we have changed as people. For others, friendships change because the environment itself is no longer the same.

For example, going to a new town, taking a promotion at a new company, or even a life change (such as becoming a mother or care-giver of an older parent) can greatly impact your friendships. But if you grew close to a friend within the confines of your daily work encounters, it may suffer tremendously once you leave. This is because your relationship never had practice in any other environment but the one where you worked.

If you have children, you'll find that while one or two friends stay close, that the level of intimacy you experience with the other women in your life significantly changes over time. This is likely because your interests, availability, priorities, and perspectives have changed.

While true intimacy can certainly survive new cities and new babies, it's often impacted gradually because the time you spend together decreases (and repeated exposure is one of the key elements of maintaining a relationship), which means you're likely sharing less about what's going on in your life (impacting the critical *Sharing* sector of your friendship). Intimacy can also weaken when two women adopt new mentalities and entertain new ideas that no longer allow them to support and accept each other in the same way. This does not mean the *caring* for another woman stops, but the level of desire to invest can impede what was otherwise a strong connection.

The key is to find a way to wish another woman well, check-in with her on social media, and to pray for her and her family, but to know that you can't possibly continue to invest in the relationship the way you did in another stage in your life… and that's okay. Sometimes we get frustrated because we long for things to be the way they were before, and it's simply not possible. And although the Tough-Love Friendship Model requires that you *Share, Preserve, Affirm, and Challenge*; where do you go when you no longer have the capacity to sustain the demands of that level of friendship?

ENOUGH INTIMACY TO GO AROUND?

And when intimacy changes with one friend, it may be a painful loss. But the silver-lining is that it also makes room for *more* intimacy with someone else.

Robin Dunbar is an anthropologist whose most popular contribution to the field of sociology is his theory known as the "Rule of 150." According to studies, the average person can only cognitively maintain up to 150 relationships in his or her network. Now of course all of those relationships don't take the same priority. The thought is that there is only enough "mental capacity" to engage up to 5 friends in your personal circle (and once you have a romantic partner, he learned, it takes up *two* of those five spaces).

It's not possible to sustain every relationship you enter into. This means that we have to acknowledge our closeness with people will certainly change, and our network will collectively shift over time.

So sometimes you have to know when a friendship—no matter how intimate it once was—is over.

Some of us get in trouble trying to hold so tightly to the idea of what USED to be that the current friendship suffocates, with no more room to grow or evolve.

This is an unpopular opinion, but these are the reasons why I have grown to dislike the term "best friend." I have come to realize how it can be problematic. Hear me out! There's this unspoken moment when you both realize "This is my best friend." Of all my friends you're the best one. But with that comes the unspoken set of expectations. Don't get me wrong: I love the idea of women who celebrate being so close (*We've been best friends since the third grade!*). I think it's admirable to remain so close for so long and to have reserved a special space in each other's lives on a through life's shifting stages.

But for so many of us, it can be a problem because "best" changes. It can subconsciously hold us hostage to the expectation of sharing more, doing more, and valuing more the bond with this one person over everyone else. I wonder, too, how it subconsciously limits the ways we develop closeness with others, fearful that enjoying someone new would be disloyal to our "bestie." I also wonder if it's why we struggle so much when we begin to realize she's no longer our "bestie" and we grapple with what to do now that the hierarchy we've built for ourselves has shifted (and we sometimes fight to save it).

If I'm saying you're my best friend, whether I announce it or not, there are certain things I now expect of you. And when things go contradictory to that (*we're not speaking as much as we used to*) it's more difficult to grapple with any evolution or change because anything other than harmony is a complete cognitive dissonance. We're supposed to be BFF but lately I don't *feel* like it. I avoid the term altogether.

Regardless of the reasons we fall out of (or into) friendship, the fact remains: there will be a shift in dynamics as we learn and grow as independent women. If the intimacy in your friendship has changed, I encourage you to ask yourself the following questions:

Have new beliefs affected our closeness and can we recover?

Have life circumstances gotten in the way, and are they seasonal or permanent?

Have new associations (marriage, childbirth) affected the friendship? If so, does it simply require effort to change how we operate, but not end the relationship altogether?

Am I in a mental space in life that no longer allows me to hold tight to my friend without revisiting attitudes and behaviors I've outgrown?

Has a betrayal occurred that has affected my trust with this person? Am I willing to continue the friendship and rebuild the trust, or did it outweigh the good in our friendship?

EVALUATING YOUR INTIMACY CAPACITY

You'll notice that I am not providing steps to either grow or detach from your friendships. While some of us just scream "Give me a step-by-step guide!", it wouldn't be helpful. Because each woman, her attachment style, her life season, and her network is entirely different, it's not possible to provide a one-size fits all guide for what exactly to say or do to achieve intimacy and navigate conflict.

Ultimately, we've got to do the work to become more self-aware, getting familiar with our attachment style, needs, and ability to give selflessly for someone else. Where is there room to grow? Examine the things that are getting in the way of you drawing close to other women. Spend some time thinking about how you can be accepting of other women's shortcomings in the same way you expect of them.

We all crave intimacy and closeness in our relationships; it's a natural, God-given desire. By understanding what intimacy looks like and taking inventory of our mental and emotional capacity to give and receive it, we put ourselves on the path to enjoying fruitful, tough-love friendships.

You, Me, Us: The Benefits of Tough-Love Friendship

It was the third time that week.

I tried to shrug it off and remind myself of all the very valid reasons that my best friend was cancelling on me... again.

She's super busy. She probably has stacks of papers to grade and she's really behind. Her daughter may be sick again. She's probably still struggling to bounce back after the break-up. Maybe she didn't realize we agreed to meet at 7:00???

I'd stored excuses for her the way I stashed bobby pins— putting a handful in my car and in my purse and in my bathroom, never sure of when I might need one. But somehow, just like those bobby pins, the excuses gradually vanished one by one until I didn't have any left.

We were fast friends, drawing close to each other as teachers at a low-income high school. I think we sensed that, despite the professional exteriors we were forced to wear in the hallways, there was humor and rebellion lying just beneath our professional display.

Before we got to know each other, we were always cordial but kept our distance, still unfamiliar. I think we were secretly assessing if the other was "cool" enough to let our guard down with. And then one day, while several teachers from the department were eating lunch together in the teachers' lounge, I made a joke (I was pretty proud of how clever it was but tried not to show it, pretending I was that witty all the time) and she laughed— hard.

That was the moment we both realized we would probably actually like each other, and before we knew it, we were hanging out all the time. We were baptized together and went dancing together and road tripped together and commiserated over bad dates and covered for each other at work and… it was a fast friendship. The closeness came at record speed and we laughed like you couldn't imagine.

The only problem is that she was *always* flaking. Always.

And I'd had this realization one week as she went into her third day of backing out on our plans.

It was normal for us to agree to hang out only for her to cancel at the last minute. Sometimes she'd really lean into me when things with her boyfriend were bad; but when they were good, I wouldn't hear from her. There were even two occasions when we were supposed to get together and there *wasn't even* a last-minute text. There was nothing at all. I had been, on more than one occasion, totally stood up only to receive a text 24 hours later about how she'd misplaced her phone or had fallen asleep.

For some reason, as verbal as I am, I never called her out on it. I'd just make a joke about it and we moved on. But it bothered me, and I found myself secretly growing resentful. I became snippy with her, and I rolled my eyes (more than usual), making passive aggressive comments whenever I overheard her make any kind of plan or commitment to someone else.

To see that she was totally unfazed, while I was steeped in miry frustration only made things worse.

I was fine operating in the *Sharing* and *Affirming* sectors of the Tough-Love Friendship Model, but my fear of losing her got in the way of me being able to verbalize my boundaries, specifically those surrounding being cancelled on multiple times a week (*Preserving*). I was also too nervous to call her out on her inconsiderate behavior (*Challenging*).

I wish I could tell you that I finally sat her down and told her it wasn't cool that she kept bailing on me (and everyone else, I soon discovered), but I had the suffocating fear that 1. she'd mistake me for being a clingy friend, which would touch on my insecurity that perhaps I *was* more invested in the friendship than she was; 2. she would get upset and distance herself from me altogether; and 3. it would put a screeching halt to our good times and I'd totally isolate myself.

If you're the anxious type, not knowing how this story ended is likely frustrating you right now. And it *is* frustrating. There was no resolution. I'll never know what would have happened if I'd voiced my discontent instead of inserting my own interpretations of her failed commitments. I never told her how I felt, nor did I ask her questions about what she did, and whether my thoughts were accurate.

All I know is that it created emotional distance and then, in this space of separation, I did something that (unintentionally) hurt her, and now outside of the occasional Instagram comment, we have no communication. (And, can I be honest? I miss her.)

After ten years of observing and questioning women of all ages and backgrounds, I realized that I'm not alone. This is happening among female friendships everywhere.

WHEN THE RISK OVERWHELMS US

There is a secret, private stirring within us as we wrestle with the much-too familiar predicament: address conflict with our girlfriend or leave it alone—invite her into an honest conversation about how we truly feel, or hold it all inside.

But tough-love friendship is all about doing hard things for the sake of each woman *and* the overall bond. This includes keeping each other accountable, expressing our needs and boundaries, and often times the "hard thing" takes the form of a simple conversation.

Ironically, we can have our greatest uncertainty with the people we are closest to. While there are certainly sociological, neurological, and cultural reasons we are conditioned to avoid tough conversations with other women, we must do the work to navigate this space because intimacy and connection are on the other side.

Drawing a friend close to share a hard truth is one of the most courageous acts in a friendship. It requires vulnerability on both sides: the one initiating the conversation must open up and reveal a discomfort or dissatisfaction. In doing so, she risks being misunderstood or isolated. The friend being addressed will be made vulnerable because she must listen as someone draws her into a conversation about a less-than-ideal situation, possibly touching on her secret insecurities and sensitivities.

Consider this, for example: If you decide to talk with a friend about the concerns you have about her boyfriend, you run the risk of being perceived as jealous, malicious, or judgmental. She, having been questioned about her choice of men, may feel exposed (if she was already questioning the strength of her new relationship) or embarrassed (if she is trying to make the relationship work but finds her efforts thwarted by your lack of support). And too often, the subtext is misread we fill in the gaps with our own narrative. Unable to recover from the awkwardness and misunderstanding, we avoid the effort to make it right.

Even among the closest of friends there are unspoken landmines in shadowed corners. Regardless of our history and the secrets we've shared, there is territory we're both aware of but refuse to traverse. The potential consequences are too great a risk...

To tell her you are still hurt by those things she said about the way you parent...

To reveal your disappointment in her lack of support...

To finally call her out on her racist jokes...

To confess that you feel you've outgrown each other...

How do you even begin a conversation like that? And more importantly— is it worth it?

Despite the initial risk and discomfort, it's so worth it.

When done correctly, there are three beneficiaries of tough-love friendships:
1. those who give it,
2. those who receive it,
3. and the friendships itself.

WHEN WE'RE HONEST, EVERYBODY WINS

There are certainly emotional, physiological, and relational benefits for everyone involved in a tough-love friendship.

Let's look at each.

A. The girl who gives it

For the woman who finds the courage to initiate a "tough-love moment," she will find that it nurtures and protects her own well being. She will soon be releasing anxiety (as she refuses to suppress her frustrations); avoids resentment (this often builds as we hold unspoken grudges against someone); establishing boundaries (this protects her); and has her needs met (friends can't meet your needs until you communicate them).

B. The girl who receives it

For the woman who finds herself on the receiving end of a tough truth, she finds liberation while having growth areas revealed (as her friend deliver truths she may not have been aware of about herself); has a better understanding of her friends (because a "call-out" can be, at its core, a revelation of what your friend's desires and values); get help in recovering from life's challenges (tough-love provides direction, accountability and support—things we all require for confidence and growth).

In fact, I interviewed a vibrant and friendly woman in her 40's, asking her about a time she was challenged by a friend and how it helped her.

"I had been divorced for a few years, and I'd been complaining about my ex nearly every day. Eventually one of my friends told me that I'd become the stereotypical bitter woman scorned," she recalled. *"I was devastated. I was embarrassed and thought, 'Oh my gosh, okay, that's not who I want to be.' I just thought, 'Wow.' Sometimes our friends give us negative feedback, and it may hurt. But with my friend, I knew her heart was bigger than the moment. I knew her well enough to trust she had my best interest in mind and it was coming from a genuine place."*

Tough-love gave her a perspective that she was unable to see because she was too close to the situation to understand, from an outside view, how her fixation was transforming her into a bitter person that no one wanted to be around.

C. The friendship itself

The greatest byproduct of tough-love friendship is intimacy.

As we outlined in the previous chapter, the ultimate level of closeness and understanding is possible when both women are operating in each courage sector of tough-love friendship.

EVIDENCE FOR THE NEED FOR INTIMACY

A study conducted by Duane Burhmester of the University of Texas at Dallas, examined several adolescents to determine the effects of intimacy (or perceived intimacy) on a person's "socio-emotional functioning," which is another way of saying how we cope with life's curve balls.

It turns out that the depth of closeness we have with other people is actually a critical factor in our ability to handle difficult transitional periods in our lives.

And while this study specifically analyzed young people as its subjects, it's surprising applicable to women in their 20's and 30's.

Here's why.

For Millennials, we are literally dealing with our own form of "adolescence." While traditional stages of adolescence include puberty and an overall shift from childhood to adulthood, I'd like to think Millennials deal with this on more of a cognitive level. While our bodies are not developing, our mentalities and ideologies are. The idealism we formed as young people is tested by experience. Each of the ideals we adopted in our younger years is tried by actual encounters with real life:

- We enter into careers we think we'll love only to realize our professional plans don't align with our passions and skill-sets.
- We seek housing in towns we expected to thrive in, only to be confronted by the reality of its demographics and the requirements to actually live there.
- We are forced to re-examine friendships we thought were long-term because we learn new things about ourselves (and our girlfriends) that make it impossible to move forward together.
- We find ourselves measuring the lessons we learned in school against the new ways technology has changed the landscape post-graduation—of our friendships, our communication, our social habits.

- We experience new countries and spiritual practices and strange men and are suddenly forced to re-calibrate, like a GPS route we blindly trust until we lose signal. Suddenly we have to navigate a very serious space without the road map we spent so long memorizing. We are adults by definition, but are still earning the maturity and qualifications. We're suddenly thrust into this new space and left to form new ideas, adopt new lifestyles, and test our hand-me-down beliefs. It's our own special form of adolescence. And we can't experience that kind of change alone.

If Burhmester's study examined how intimacy among young people determined their ability to emotionally manage the "changes of life," then it's even *more* necessary for the actual CHANGES OF LIFE we encounter in our 20s and 30s, when we're making serious, long-term decisions about family, love, and work. It's even more critical to have deep and meaningful friendships when we are becoming mothers and getting married and divorced and starting new jobs and moving to new cities to chase new beginnings.

Here are some highlights taken directly from his journal article "Intimacy of Friendship, Interpersonal Competence, and Adjustment During Preadolescence and Adolescence," along with my personal applications to female Millennial friendship:

First, not having intimate friends may be a significant source of stress. Harry Stack Sullivan argued that the need for intimacy intensifies during early adolescence, and if left unsatisfied through friendship, leads to heightened feelings of loneliness, alienation, and depression.

[A recent survey of more than one thousand Millennials found that they are more lonely than any other generation. This is due largely in part to a culture that makes it hard for us to pursue deep and meaningful friendships, enjoying the kind of intimacy that would make us feel connected and supported. Research also shows that women report greater feelings of loneliness than men. With the intersection of women and Millennials, this becomes an especially critical subject for female friendships.]

Second, adolescents appear to have an increased desire for self-disclosure and self-exploration rooted in a need for "consensual validation" of personal worth (Parker & Gottman, 1989; Sullivan, 1953). Youths who do not have intimate friendships may miss out on important validating interactions, which can leave them feeling less secure, more anxious, and less worthy.

[Millennial female friendships require this more than ever as they work to make sense of their changing world. The political climate, technology, and social norms are so different from what we knew. We are also trying on new roles of "mother" and "manager" and "wife" and learning how to operate with our parents from this new space of adulthood. We *need* people to validate these experiences if we expect to survive — and thrive— in them.]

Finally, youths who lack intimate friendships may be deprived of important sources of social support and coping assistance. The support of intimate friends may be particularly important during adolescence as the young person confronts a variety of uniquely adolescent stressors (e.g., bodily changes, sexuality, dating, and strained family relationships), many of which cannot comfortably be discussed with parents.

[This has strong applications to those in their 20's and 30's as they may find that certain associates are not suitable for vulnerable self-disclosure. Where adolescents feel unable to reveal certain things to their parents, Millennial women find that there is much to be lost or misunderstood if divulging to co-workers or even romantic partners. There are spaces uniquely reserved for friendship— close, female friendship— where "coping assistance" is most readily available.]

When a woman initiates a tough love conversation, she initiates a shift in the relationship itself. The pressure! But what if that shift wasn't a bad thing? What if that shift was just what you need to enter into a personal freedom and draw closer to your friend?

We can achieve this kind of intimacy and closeness. We can achieve this level of understanding, wholeheartedness and acceptance. But, contrary to what our culture would have us believe, it does not come through "niceness" and safe assurances. It does not come with polite exchanges and withheld frustrations.

But, there *is* something getting in the way.

THE CONSEQUENCE OF SILENCE: CUT-OFF CULTURE

Now that we understand the different levels of intimacy and how tough-love friendships allow us to achieve the highest level of closeness, let's look at one of the very real downsides of life without that level of intimacy.

A lack of tough-love friendships has given birth to a new epidemic: Cut-off culture.

Cut-off culture refers to the increasingly accepted practice of completely ending communication with someone without warning or explanation. It has always been commonplace in the dating world: after a date (or two) with someone she's no longer interested in, a woman may stop returning phone calls and avoiding places she knows she might see the guys she's dodging. It is not unusual for women to opt out of romantic relationships or prospects when they've been offended or feel there's no chemistry.

But it doesn't end there.

Women have also begun incorporating this tendency in their personal friendships.

We turn to cut-off culture as a means of dealing with a situation we don't know how to handle. Things get messy and confusing and we lack the confidence and skill to have hard conversations, stand up for ourselves, and call our friends out on toxic behaviors.

We opt-in to cut-off culture when we've been offended or misunderstood. We choose to ghost other women when we decide that moving forward would be too hard.

Perhaps it's also an extension of that "Tinder swipe" mentality so many of us have adopted. Some of us just feel that it would be easier to make a new friend rather than "figure things out" with ones we have. Like a dating app, we mentally "swipe right" with ease, knowing there are tons of options on the other side. (Don't get me wrong, I'm not knocking dating apps— I met my husband that way so... yay swiping!)

After ten years of examining friendships among women ages 16 to 55, I can confidently say that cut-off culture wouldn't be as prevalent if we knew how to be a better friend. The danger of avoiding tough conversations is that it can lead to complete avoidance altogether. While it may seem like an immediate and relatively harmless solution, it can actually be damaging. While the "cut-off" queen gets relief and resolution, the friend getting jilted is left wondering what she did wrong, internalizing the disappearance, and dealing with rejection.

What may be an "out" for one is a lack of closure for another.

This is problematic because it could impact the "ghosted" woman's willingness to operate within the *Sharing* and *Challenging* courage sectors of the Tough-Love Friendship Model in her future relationships. Working to understand why she was abandoned and where she went wrong, she'll likely wrestle with ideas like "Did I overshare? Did I say something she didn't like? Did I offend her?"

WHEN YOU'RE THE ONE WHO'S "GHOSTED"

Let's reverse roles for a moment. Instead of putting yourself in the place of the one who is "ghosting," I want you to pause for a second to recall a time you were socializing pretty regularly with a girl (or sometimes, a group of girls) and for some reason or another, they stopped talking to you.

I mean, really— pause here for a moment and scroll through your memory files. You may not even have to go back that far. Do you currently have anyone in your life who you haven't spoken to in a while— who sends text responses days (or weeks?!) later, if at all? Lack of response is a lighter form of ghosting— delayed and minimal response after formerly being highly engaged.

It's definitely happened to me. And I've been guilty of doing it to others.

WHEN YOU'RE THE ONE DOING THE "GHOSTING"

I wish I could say that the days of girls "icing each other out" ends in high school, but we all know that's not the case. I was reminded of that very recently…

I'm in a small networking group that meets once a month to chat about business. There are about ten women involved, and although it began as a professional thing, many of us quickly grew close.

Our most recent outing was at a fancy Mediterranean lounge, and I found myself in the restroom with a few of the other women. Per usual, we congregated and began to chat.

As one of our many laugh-fests trickled down, the conversation fell to a hush as one woman made a confession:

"Can I tell you something? One of the new girls is not my favorite person She's loud and thinks she knows everything. So I've been thinking...we should start another networking group and not invite her— like, let's start a new group text and everything and just leave her off."

She searched our faces to find a partner for her plotting.

We responded with confused laughter, wondering if she was serious. As she held her gaze, we realized that she was gauging our willingness to conspire with her. It took me a while because I was stunned, and I searched for a way to let her know it wasn't cool without embarrassing her.

"I mean, I don't know specifically who you're talking about, but I actually like all the girls. Even the ones I don't totally click with— it's just cool to have different personalities, don't you think? I don't wanna ice anyone out..."

Uneasily, she responded, "Yeah, I mean I guess."

And I still wonder what would have happened had we agreed, forming a new group text and meeting secretly to throw the new girl off our trail. Honestly, maybe they did it anyway and left me out of the group text, too! Ha!

But seriously, that woman would've wondered why we vanished, and instead of learning that she came across as judgmental and that her comments were sometimes too harsh, she'd be left to grapple with the fact that she'd been cut-off, and trying to figure out why.

I know this sounds like an extreme example, to plan to form a new group to avoid one woman, but we live out our own versions of this every day. The friend who says something weird or that offends us or who simply hasn't been us giving "good vibes" lately— we cut her off. And in some cases, we brag about it. But in reality, the cut-off really speaks to our lack of connection in the first place, otherwise how can you so easily withdraw from the relationship? It also points to our inability or unwillingness to communicate our discomfort and our incapacity for conflict and/or awkwardness.

We all know this story too well because, unequipped and unprepared, we turn to cut-off culture rather than become tough-love friends. Rather than tell a woman, "Hey, I was turned off by what you said the other day" or "I don't know if I have the time to really invest right now," we bail.

In years past, an unwanted friendship may have at least been mildly sustained with a few pleasantries, but in a world where there are hundreds of ways to connect, we can access each other in more ways than ever which means "ghosting" hits even harder.

Abrupt relational withdrawal both feeds and enables our discomfort with real, honest "tough love" conversations. We've made it far too easy to retreat and replace. We've made it far too easy to opt out.

And this only contributes to our collective issues with abandonment, attachment, rejection, and vulnerability.

The benefits of tough-love friendship?

Connection in the midst of misunderstanding. Trust in knowing that your friends will be honest with you. Comfort in a relationship where you can communicate freely— no guessing games.

The benefits of tough-love friendships include open and compassionate talks. The freedom to hold tight to our boundaries and a dedication to keeping our friends accountable. Intimacy and closeness, understanding and acceptance— it all comes from tough love friendship.

When Culture Holds Us Back

Although we'd like to think we are aware of and therefore immune to societal pressures, the truth is that in order to maintain certain norms and to function alongside our peers, co-workers, and friends, we're sometimes no match for years of conditioning.

American women face a whole slew of pressures and expectations from their culture, and while there is more open dialogue now than ever before about double-standards and gender norms, the same old cultural pressures persist. Sadly, it affects everything from how we perceive each other to the language we use when we talk to (or about) each other. It's woven so deeply into our thoughts and behavior that it's difficult to completely extract gender bias from our day-to-day lives.

When I took psychology classes in undergrad, I learned about the two kinds of gender bias. One is prescriptive and the other is descriptive. Basically, descriptive bias refers to the way we describe women, including qualities we just assume they naturally have. You see this at play when people generally describe women as caring, modest, compassionate, sensitive, and feminine. Seems harmless enough, right? But prescriptive bias is when we penalize women for not living up to the expectations we have of them: "Women are *supposed to be* feminine, so why is she being so rough?"

For example, if our culture believes women are passive, then when she asks for a pay raise, we think she is being too forward.

Do you see how this is a total lose-lose?

If we collectively believe that women are modest (descriptive), then we'll be turned off when she talks about her accomplishments, viewing it instead as boastful and unladylike (prescriptive).

The problem with bias is more obvious in a work setting. The evidence for financial, social, and professional double-standards is a mammoth testament to the need for change.

But how does gender bias affect our female friendships?

Sadly, it's not just men who subscribe to these thoughts and expectations about women. We do it to each other. And I don't think it's malicious— in fact, most bias isn't. It's just incredibly dangerous when it goes unchecked.

When we believe falsities about our own gender, our friendships will suffer for it. If we believe women to be catty and drama-prone, then we'll be more likely to dismiss opportunities to work through hard things, writing it off with a *"This is why I can't deal with women— too much drama!"*

The ramifications of believing negative stereotypes has an obvious impact on our relationship with other women. But what if it's not only the *negative* stereotypes that are affecting our ability to be real with each other?

HOW GENDER BIAS PLAYS A ROLE

Gender bias makes the very idea of "tough-love friendship" disruptive in a culture that has expectations of how women should behave and engage with each other. Remember, we are defining "tough-love friendship" as doing hard things, keeping each other accountable, and having uncomfortable conversations. On the surface this sounds like something an average, reasonable person would agree with, but we let female stereotypes get in the way of us actually demonstrating tough-love in our friendships.

Let's take a look at some cultural female expectations and the way each interferes with our connection to other women.

GENDER BIAS #1. Women are accepting.

There is this idea that women are naturally receptive and agreeable. Now of course we know too many women to think this is true, but the idea here is that we subconsciously believe these to be qualities that come naturally to women; by extension we expect them to be present in our dealings with women. When she in any way deviates from being that accepting and agreeable person that she *should* be, we perceive her as difficult.

Here's how this affects our friendships:

If we expect someone to be accepting and understanding *because she's a girl*, then when she voices her disapproval for something it is unattractive. When telling my girlfriend that her fickleness is not cool and I need her to be a little more reliable, it can be perceived as cold and intolerant.

But picture that scenario with a man, instead. We'd accept his "call-out" as being direct, as something men "just do." It would affirm our descriptive bias of men as to-the-point and assertive.

That quality on a woman, however? Bleh.

So this works two ways: Sometimes when we are called out by a female friend who is checking us on something she doesn't support or won't allow, we may find it off-putting, and it creates this wedge between us because we can't wrap our minds around a female being so "unaccepting." As friends— as female friends— aren't we supposed to fulfill the "I have your back no matter what" rah-rah? If I tell her there are things I can't accept from her or from our friendship, then am I abandoning that unspoken mantra? Am I defying some kind of girl code? Or am I setting boundaries so that she and I can function together in a way that allows the both people in the relationship to feel comfortable and respected?

We don't only exercise this bias when experiencing "un-acceptance" with our friends, but we live up to the stereotype by suppressing our desire to *express* our discontent in a friendship for fear of being perceived exactly the same way.

GENDER BIAS #2: Women are loyal.

This is an extension of the previous stereotype. Women are expected to be the more loyal gender (consider how many women remain in relationships with men after the man has strayed compared to men who choose to do the same thing). Perhaps it's because we do connect and value faithfulness, but either way the expectation can work against us in our friendships.

For those of us who buy in to the idea of women dutifully committing to the people in their lives (friends, family), we either A. unintentionally expect our friends to display their loyalty by agreeing with us, or B. let the fear of being perceived as disloyal prevent us from speaking our truth.

GENDER BIAS #3: Women are nurturing.

As the only gender able to give birth, we associate the domesticated idea of nurturing with women. Historically, yes, we have been relegated to the role of a gatherer, remaining close to home and providing sustenance to those we care for. But because of this biological assignment, there is a rampant expectation that women be these soft and gentle caregivers.

Often characterized as the more nurturing gender, women are charged with the expectation of showing gentleness to others. This kind of bias plays a role in our friendships as we work to show (the stereotypical idea of) gentleness and nurturing to our friends when they are misguided or when our friendship is suffering. If our girl is completely wildin' out, are we supposed to softly say, "Oh my gosh girl, are you okay? What's the matter? I'm here for you." or do we have the boldness to say, "Girl, that's enough. You're better than this— let's go." Yes, different situations call for the appropriate tone, but you hear what I'm saying: Passiveness is associated with femininity, and it's to the detriment of our friendships.

GENDER BIAS #4: Women should be likable.

For women, there is a premium on politeness. Although in recent years, we've grown increasingly comfortable with speaking up for ourselves, we're still mindful of how doing so is bucking the system and will make us look rude.

When men say something impolite it's typically attributed to their nature— *"He can't help it, he's a guy.... You know how guys are..."* — this gives men the freedom to offer commentary without pretext or apology. Women, however, are frequently expected to be polite. And good lord, the mental exhaustion and emotional demand of being "nice" all day…

- Smiling back to a guy who whistles at you instead of rolling your eyes because you want to be verbally assaulted

- Bringing something in for the potluck even though you don't want to/can't afford to
- Allowing someone to hug you, when in reality it makes you uncomfortable
- Offering to move your seat on a plane if someone asks to sit next to the window
- Telling the stylist your new haircut looks just fine, only to cry when you're alone in the car (no? Just me?)
- Engaging in a full conversation with a co-worker about her weekend even though you are behind on deadline

But if a woman offers something with push-back, she risks being perceived as impolite. According to Deborah Cihonski, a psychologist who studied at the University of South Florida and now practices in Illinois, women suffer from a phenomenon known as "Loss of Voice," where they begin silencing themselves once they approach adolescence. The study titled "The Experience of Loss of Voice in Adolescent Girls: An Existential-Phenomenological Study" explores firsthand accounts of girls and reasons they keep silent.

She interviewed several girls between the ages of 12 to 16, asking them to recall a time they had something important to say but did not say it. They described their situations in great detail and Cihonski boiled the top reasons down to feeling they had "so much to lose;" the second was being seen as "different," "bitchy," or "complaining;" the third was a desire to be seen as "good," and caring deeply about others' comfort more than their own.

I have seen this play out in boardrooms, night clubs, Bible studies, and restaurants. But there was no place more prominent than in the classroom.

HOW IT PLAYS OUT IN THE CLASSROOM

When I was teaching 12th-graders, I often let them choose their own partners for groups projects because although the goal was to create something together and learn how to collaborate productively, I still wanted it to be somewhat enjoyable. (It was also an "out" for me because if there were complaints later, I could always say, "I didn't pick your group mates; you did.")

It was common for students to come to me one-on-one to talk about struggles they were having with their partner. Sure, they were thrilled the day the project was assigned and just *knew* it would be the best thing ever. But it never failed that when two girls *who were friends* decided to be partners, one would address me when the other wasn't around (during her lunch period or hang back after class) to tell me what the trouble was. Most time it was about having to do most of the work or about the friend talking the project in a direction she didn't want to go in.

One situation I clearly recall is talking to a student named Megan. After the bell had rung and her classmates shuffled out of the room, she told her friend she'd catch-up with her later. Then she slowly walked to my desk, making sure everyone else was gone.

"Um, so… Joy is my friend and everything but she's not doing anything for our group project. She doesn't come when we meet in the library. And if she *does* her portion of the work she does it wrong, and when you give us class time she just plays around on her phone. I'm kinda doing everything by myself, and I don't want to get a bad grade because of her. Like, she's gonna ruin our project."

She turned red with frustration.

Having heard this complaint several times over, I gave her a knowing look and said, "I'm sorry to hear that, Megan. Sometimes it works out that way in a group: one person does the majority of the work while everyone kind of coasts through, and I guess the group has made you that person. But it shouldn't be that way."

Her shoulders relaxed as she was relieved to find validation for her concerns.

Then I asked her plainly, "So why don't you just tell her? Tell her that you need her to step up because you're worried about your grade…"

Megan's eyes grew to three times their size as she looked at me with disbelief. "I can't do that! She's my friend! Do you know how much she would hate me? No, seriously Miss. She'll … she'll tell everyone to hate me."

We worked out an arrangement that involved me confronting Joy's laziness in a crafty way that didn't let on to who told on her, and eventually everything worked out.

But it spoke to a larger issue.

I stepped in to be the "bad guy" and help the group get back on course. Everything was fine once I did. But how many of us are wishing someone *else* would step in to deliver a message without "outing" us? How many times have we just prayed that somebody else would say something so we didn't have to deal with the repercussions secretly awaiting women who speak their minds?

SPEAKING UP AS RESISTANCE

Even when we do begin to speak up, we do it with 50 million "I'm sorry but's" attached and self-defeating phrases like, "Maybe I'm just crazy, but…" to apologize for the (very valid) thing we have to say. This is why there is so much literature that has emerged recently surrounding women and their tendency to over-apologize. To say or do anything that will be remotely perceived as rude is a tightrope women walk every day.

This is why operating in the *Challenging* courage sector of the Tough-Love Friendship Model is so difficult. It's about so much more than providing accountability to a friend or sharing our feelings. It's about resistance to the very system that made it so damn difficult in the first place. We have to fight every day when we go out into the world: fight double standards, fight sexist expectations, fight our nature in order to be accepted. But we shouldn't have to do that when we're with our girls.

When we're with our girls, we should be able to share, preserve, affirm, and challenge with freedom from judgement.

Once we do, female friendship itself will be an act of resistance against the patriarchy.

Sociology is a Mother

It's not just cultural pressures that make it hard for us to be our full selves in our friendships.

It's freaking sociology, too.

On the most basic human level, we have a need to form relationship. Think back to the first time you heard of Maslow's Hierarchy of Needs— you know, the pyramid figure you stared at in your high school or college psychology textbook? For those who erased the memory: Abraham Maslow was an American psychologist who proposed this (pretty widely accepted) theory that the needs near the top of the hierarchy can't be fulfilled if the more basic needs— those appearing near the base of the triangle— aren't satisfied first. After physiological needs like water and safety needs like health, the very next need is for belonging which apparently one of the most fundamental requirements for us to eventually "self-actualize".

Is it any wonder that once we've formed a "tribe" that we do what we can to maintain our place in it? And forget the IG-worthy picture of ten girls shouting #SquadGoals. A sense of belonging can form with as few as two people who give each other a sense of purpose and connection. And when we find it, we do not want to let it go.

Although we are sociologically prone to seek relationship, some of us value belonging so much, that we will:

- Endure friends' toxic friendships
- Remain silent when women we love make jokes or comments that are

inappropriate
- Refuse to share our needs, desires, and boundaries for fear we'll be rejected

And some of us have experienced a deep and powerful loneliness, and we'll do anything not to experience it again.

I want to hover here for a second to give you a few things you can do to feel less lonely, because the fear of loneliness is so powerful that it drives some of our behavior. We'll remain in a "friendship" that's not good for us because we tell ourselves "Well, it's better than being alone." We'll avoid the pursuit of strong and healthy friendships because we don't want to be by ourselves.

HOW TO MANAGE LONELINESS SO YOU DON'T SETTLE IN FRIENDSHIP

Let me first address ways to *not* feel lonely, so that you don't think you have to tolerate empty friendships. Let me give you four ways you can quell the pain of loneliness:

1. Hold up the Target Line.

One misconception about loneliness is that the solution is to make more friends. But that's not necessarily true.

Loneliness isn't about a lack of friends—it's about a lack of connection.

If you're an introvert and the idea of attending events to make friends sends an anxious thrill up your spine, then consider engaging the everyday people around you. I challenge women to start small by sustaining the conversation with their barista, bank teller, or Target cashier by just one more minute. Simply making eye contact with your neighbor and then introducing yourself can instantly make you feel less lonely. Try to resist the temptation to hide behind your phone, and instead, maximize your interactions with the everyday people you meet.

2. Don't quit on yoga.

The most common suggestion for combating loneliness is "Join a club! Take a class!" and this is still the best way to meet people. But there is one point that people fail to make: The trick is not in going to yoga class; the key is to *keep* going.

One key ingredient in the formation of new friendships is repeated exposure.

Too often, we'll try something new in an effort to meet new people, and we set strict expectations: "If I don't make friends when I go tonight, I'm not going anymore." But when our initial class doesn't immediately result in instant-friendships, we grow discouraged and resolve to stay home next time. But I encourage you to 1. Keep attending the class and 2. Engage once you're there. Introduce yourself to people around you before your yoga class. Find a girl in spin and before you walk in, ask her if she's done it before. Then make a joke about how nervous you are and suggest she sit next to you to help you figure it out. Whatever you do, don't stop going. Give new friendship a chance by showing up each and every week.

3. Put your phone away.

Decrease your time on social media. Seriously. While social media has become the scapegoat for many of our current emotional ails, it's not without reason. Several studies now link sadness, anxiety, and overall dissatisfaction for one's life to her use of social media.

This doesn't have to be an extreme adjustment. But where you'd normally take a 30-minute scroll before bed, opt to read a book instead, or reorganize your jewelry. Really. One of the worst time to be active on social media is before bed. It increases anxiety and depression, and sends you to sleep with thoughts that are sadder than you'd have if you'd abstained.

4. Keep perspective.

It's critical to remember that loneliness is a feeling, something that will pass with time. If you hold fast to the truth that loneliness is a part of the human experience, that will help you to gain perspective. The most dangerous thing you can do is to begin to think you're only person who's feeling the way you do, or to confuse your loneliness with your self-worth. Instead of thinking "I feel lonely, but I know that things will change soon," many begin to think

"Why am I lonely? Is it because I'm not interesting or likable? What's wrong with me? Why don't I have more friends?"

Keep heart. Seasons of loneliness can spur you to necessary introspection. But it's not a mark of who you are, just where you are for a period of time.

When you're lonely, it's nice to know that you're not alone in feeling that way.

Look for ways to stay connected to the world around you, and you'll slowly feel more attached, more seen, and more in union with the people all around you.

You'll never experience true, tough love friendship if you're withholding your truth out of fear of being alone. Perhaps if more of us knew how to be content in our "aloneness," we'd have the confidence to reveal our whole selves in our relationships.

Tough-love friendship confronts difficult issues for the sake of stronger women and a stronger bonds overall. It delights in belonging and agreement, but has the courage to address hard things.

It's almost a paradoxical idea: rocking the boat to keep it afloat, but that is ultimately what tough-love friendship does. Yet despite the freedom, intimacy, and healing that lie just beneath the surface of a tough-love truth-telling, we'll avoid the conversation because we convince ourselves that it will disrupt the ecosystem we've created in that relationship, and we're scared of losing what we have.

DRIVEN BY THE NEED TO BELONG

Though most of us aren't walking around wearing a *Fear-of-Abandonment* inscribed necklace, we know it lives quietly and discreetly in the back of our minds. You'd think the need to belong would be strongest in middle school and high school, but it's actually more important than ever once we begin to navigate the end of our 20's and we've hit (or are striving to enter) major, ground-shifting chapters. We are giving birth and getting married and gaining roles of authority in our jobs, moving away from the town we love (or hate), finally exploring faith for ourselves instead of subsisting on the religion that was handed down to us.

Confronting a girlfriend with something difficult is so petrifying because it seems almost counterintuitive. One of our primary sociological needs is to feel like we belong. When we come across a group that welcomes, embraces, and understands us, we feel like we are "home." Connecting with a group of women who welcome you, enjoy your company, and make you feel understood is a joy like no other. And bringing up a topic that could possibly revoke your acceptance into a group that likes you— well, that just feels silly.

Child welfare veteran, Amelia Franck Meyer, describes this natural desire for acceptance in her Tedx Talk "The Human Need for Belonging":

"We come into the world, literally tethered to another human being. And that need for claiming and belonging never goes away our whole life long. We must belong to thrive and survive, we must be part of a human family, part of a tribe, in order to feel safe and protected... Connection is not the same as being claimed. Your connections may be many. But you are only claimed by a precious few."

Meyer so eloquently explains why that drive to find groups that accept us is so strong. But with a hunger for that deep sense of belonging, we're sometimes unwilling to bring our full selves the table. But remember, the third level of intimacy is where both people can bring their full selves to the relationship, which means diverging opinions are welcome.

Tough-love friendship requires that you show up in every way as your authentic, uncensored self— especially in times of disagreement. Disagreement doesn't have to mean discord. But bringing your honesty to a friendship is the only way to really truly find your people and experience the kinds of intimacy you're craving.

If there's a part of you that can't shake the anxiety-inducing idea of confronting a friend, remember that it is totally natural. You are wired to want to belong. God *designed* us to connect with others. But expressing discontent— by saying "Hey, something isn't right"— can erect invisible walls that slowly but firmly box us out, and keep us from enjoying the comforting attachments we've formed.

FEAR OF ISOLATION

The need to maintain relationship is so strong that many of us hold on to unhealthy bonds for the sake of having an attachment to something, anything. On the other side of belonging is isolation. And I am even of the belief that loneliness affects women differently than it does men. We value our friendships so much because they involve our invested emotion, connection through socializing, and secret-keeping— it's like grieving a break-up when it doesn't work out because we give so much of ourselves. It makes sense that we'd want to work to avoid a life without that connection, thrusting some of us into situations where we remain friends with the wrong women for too long.

And it's primal. A woman without a group is vulnerable prey. She doesn't enjoy the safety and security of a pack, and alone she is completely doomed. But we can't prioritize our sociological need to belong over our individual well-being. Ironically, finding the courage to voice how we really feel and what we really need moves us closer to the right people.

A GLIMPSE OF BELONGING AFTER 50

The work that I've done exploring female friendships has largely focused on ladies ages 16 to 55. Curious to see if the dynamics and nuance I've observed would look different among an older group of women, I interviewed a group of ten elderly women who crochet as fiber artists. The group meets regularly at the local bookstore (the one I visited weekly as I wrote this book), and I asked them if I could have a conversation with them about connection among women.

They agreed.

Here is the adapted transcript:

Q: Can you tell me what you ladies do when you come together?
A: (Joyce, mid-50's) We've met for the past two years to chat with each other on different styles and methods [of crocheting], and we show off our work to each other. But mostly, we just talk. It's nice to have a group you see every week and you can

just talk and laugh together.

Q: Could you ladies tell me how you each learned of the group and why you're here?

A: (Janice, mid-50's) I'm a retired teacher from Pennsylvania. I've been here in Florida for three years and I keep coming to this group because it's so hard to meet new people. And I mean, I don't want to go on one of those dating sites. I don't want make company, even though my daughter keeps telling me to go for it. But I just want some lady friends, thank you very much.

A: (Debra mid-60's) I lived in West Palm. My husband died 4 years ago and I moved in with my daughter. I've only been coming to the crochet group for three months, but I need this. It's nice to have other ladies to talk to. And I was getting arthritis. But since I've been coming? No arthritis!

Q: So as you knit, what do you ladies talk about? How often do you just talk about the craft, and how often do you talk about other things?

A: (Joyce) Oh, we talk about craft about 20% time. But most times we talk about our kids or husbands or other random things. Like, one time we were talking about kilts and we were wondering if the guys wear anything underneath... we found out that they don't. We can be pretty naughty, I guess.

(Doris, late 60's) Yeah, it's an "Education" group— write that down!

(Joyce) We also do charities, we like to give to others. But we don't talk about politics or religion. And we support each other. One woman recently lost her family member. And we were there for her.

(Michelle mid 60's) It's our therapy to come here. One woman in the group has a physical challenge but she takes the bus to get here every week. It takes her three hours here and three hours back. That's how important this group is to us.

(Doris) We have formed a friendship over the time. I look forward to Saturdays. I belong to another group, but this one is more fun.

(Martha, mid 50's) I think the size is important too. I also belong to a travel group... and three different choral groups and all we talk about is music. And I've been to other group.. but this is my favorite. I can be myself here.

As I spoke with the ladies I realized that struggling to find your "people" is not just something unique to adolescents or Millennials. It's a challenge that we face during any life transition. And these older women, with their girl-like squeals and dentured smiles were so happy to have found a group to belong to as they lost spouses, retired, and yearned for connection in their new season.

The conversation weaved from one subject to the other, dancing colorfully and intertwining in sync with their hands and the yarn they were weaving. And as we continued to chat, they forgot that I was there and began recalling stories, laughing with each other, and reveling in the joy of having sister circle to belong to. I eventually put my pencil and paper down and just watched them, and quietly slipped away to let them to continue to enjoy each other.

Inspired by their tenderness, I jumped in my car and called up the women *I* am proud to "belong" to. And I pray we stay connected into the years of old age.

I Feel Your Pain (and Other Crazy Wiring)

"I don't want to hurt her feelings."

Can you think back to the last time you said that? And if you haven't murmured those exact words then surely you've at least had the sentiment: a fear of speaking your mind and making someone feel bad in the process.

You're not alone.

It turns out that one of the primary reasons we struggle with direct confrontation in our friendships is because we're neurologically wired to consider her feelings— and we're socially conditioned to put those feelings above our own. While empathy is an incredibly powerful attribute, it can sometimes work to our detriment.

There's a reason why "tough love" conversations give us so much pause: our brains are literally fashioned in a way that makes us uniquely sensitive to others' emotions. We've heard time and time again about how women are the more empathetic gender.

HOW YOUR BRAIN GETS IN THE WAY

To put this thought to the test, but Leonardo Christov-Moore (who studied psychiatry at UCLA) and Dr. Marco Iacoboni (director of UCLA's Neuromodulation Lab) conducted a study to learn the truth. There had been tons of scientific studies examining whether or not females were the more sympathetic gender, but until these men looked into it, there hadn't been a study using brain imaging.

Here's what they did.

To see if there was actually neurological proof that women are more empathetic than men, they took several participants of each gender and scanned them one by one through an MRI. While each lay still in the machine, the men and women were shown two different videos.

One video showed a soft cotton swab making contact with the palm of a hand. As you can imagine, there wasn't much increased brain activity in response to that visual.

But then Christov-Moore and Dr. Iacoboni showed each participant a video of a large needle going into the palm of a hand (I can seriously picture it right now and I'm cringing). While both genders generally showed higher brain activity for this video than the cotton swab video, the women's brain activity went through the roof. There was some monitoring of blood-oxygen levels to gauge just how much women were "feeling" the pain of the person in the video, but the process is beyond my scope of expertise (but it's available on UCLA's online study archives if you want to dig in— fascinating stuff).

When women say "I feel your pain," apparently we mean it.

So what does this have to do with having tough conversations with our friends?

We're so connected to each others' pain and emotional experiences that when we envision the awkwardness, embarrassment, or anger she may feel, we can almost tangibly feel her emotional pain. Our ability to picture her response, and then sympathize with it, causes us to avoid the confrontation altogether.

Thinking "Well, I don't want to make her feel bad," we do all we can to circumvent the issue instead of dealing with it head-on— that is, despite all we know intellectually about how not saying *anything* can actually end up being a bigger problem.

The anxiety of just *imagining* how uncomfortable she may be is almost just as bad as *seeing* her actual discomfort during our conversation. Typically, once women have mustered the courage to say what they feel, they'll see their friend's embarrassment or anger and change course. This usually comes in the form of apologies or minimizing statements like "But... I mean, what do I know. I might just be over-thinking it," or "I'm sorry, I could be wrong..." completely pivoting away from the initial message.

The subject of our "tough-love" conversation sometimes isn't even monumental.

Recently, a friend of mine dropped by unannounced. I think back in the day I would have welcomed it, but now that I'm married I try to be more mindful of how some things I used to do may need adjusting. When she knocked on the door, I was surprised— the house was a mess, I'd had a long day at work, and the baby was fussy. It simply wasn't a good time. But I let her in and managed to chat for a bit before hinting that I needed to put the baby down and get ready for bed.

I called another friend after it happened: "I love her, but that really caught me off guard. I don't think I can do the whole drop-in thing anymore."

She answered me simply: "Yeah, I know what you mean. Just tell her."

It's funny because this was during the time I was writing this book. As I'm advising women to be bolder in their friendships, here I was having to practice what I was preaching! In bed that night, I'll admit: I was a little worried about how she'd take it, imagining her getting offended or mistaking my boundaries for thinking I'm "too good" to operate the way I used to. I called her up the next day and we caught-up on work before I let her know about my new boundaries:

"Hey, girl, real quick... about yesterday: Just shoot me a text or something before you roll through because I can't give you my best if you just pop in. And you never know what could be happening over here, its' always so unpredictable. So... you cool with calling beforehand?" I felt her pause as I tried my best to remain even-keeled, casual. A little thrown off she agreed, "Oh! Uh, yeah, that's cool, my bad."

We went for drinks the next day, laughing wildly about anything and everything. We recovered. Our history, mutual respect, and love offered us a space to express our boundaries without worry of being abandoned or misunderstood by the other.

It looks like I was able to work past my brain's nature to make me fixate on her potential discomfort.

WHEN CULTURE WIRES OUR RESPONSES

This is more than a neurological attribute—it's cultural, too. We find it noble when a woman puts others above herself. Again, it totally is! But not to the extent of crippling self-sacrifice. Not to the point of ongoing self-detriment. We have been taught that making ourselves small so that others can be fulfilled is just a woman's duty. **We find it admirable and call it "selflessness."**

The trouble is we carry this responsibility into our roles as friends. Even when a friend begins doing things that we're not cool with— even when a friendship has become toxic, we find it difficult to confront her because we either justify it by empathizing with her ("I don't want to make her uncomfortable…"); speculating about what the confrontation might do to her ("What if she gets upset and can't bounce back…?"); and in every other way elevating (and oftentimes, exaggerating) her potential discomfort with us delivering our truth. Even when it comes to our detriment— even when the alternative is to hold our peace and accept the current dynamic, no matter how ill-fashioned— we are tempted to elevate her comfort above our own well being.

To be clear, at the heart of it, these are reasonable, even virtuous considerations.

To sacrifice our comfort for someone else's is noble, on the surface. But what is sacrifice when it comes at the cost of our mental or emotional health? The sacrifice becomes masochism; the over-empathizing becomes self-harm.

There's a TEDxTalk by Sheila Norgate, a visual artist, performer, and feminist. It's titled "Trouble on the Homefront," and in her speech, she so eloquently articulates what many of us know but struggle to explain: We are *too* empathic.

Every time I watch this video, it knocks the wind out of me. Norgate says:

"A woman can be too empathic. She can be dangerously empathic. And I believe that we've been in training for this hazardous work since before the dead sea was

even sick. Somewhere along the line, a perfectly good idea that we should all be thoughtful and considerate went straight off the rails where women and girls are concerned, and veered into oncoming traffic and there at the side of the road in the smoking twisted wreckage can be found the discarded footwear of those of us who fled the scene wearing someone else's shoes.

How did this happen?

How did being considerate and kind and being able to put yourself in someone else's place how did his turn into a calling? A vocation? Something women will be willing to aspire to at any cost?.... We need to make sure somehow women and girls remain in their own shoes long enough to break them in before wandering off in someone else's. And this way is the only way empathy becomes what it is really meant to be— an inside job."

But how do we get past it?

Here are a few ways we can stop our "over-sympathizing" from immobilizing us when it's time to share hard truths (about our friend or about ourselves):

1. **Acknowledge her feelings and perspective.** Tough love doesn't mean saying, "I don't care how she feels. I'm gonna tell her how I feel." Instead, it has the attitude of "I care so much about her feelings that I'll be mindful of them as I share what's on my heart."

2. **Lead with your own vulnerability.** If you're broaching a subject that could embarrass her, then start by commiserating. Create connection when you anticipate her feeling rejected or called out. While you have control over the tenderness and tone with which you communicate a tough truth, you can't help how it may make her feel. Try beginning the conversation establishing common ground to minimize your fixation on how she might feel. Control what you can.

3. **Stay present.** Try to resist the temptation to spiral and extrapolate. Yeah, she may initially misunderstand your message, get defensive, or push back, but try not to apologize for speaking up to absolve her of discomfort. Don't silence yourself. Check that you're speaking with compassion, and stay in the now, not obsessing over the fear that she *may* leave or how she *may* twist the message you shared or how she *might* get mad. Just be present.

4. **Remember what's on the other side.** When you have something to say that may not be well-received at first, try to remember the reason you *are* speaking up in the first place. You may want to stop the frustration you're experiencing over being silent. You may be sitting on a truth that she needs to hear but no one else is brave enough to share it with her. You may need to say what's on your heart for your own healing or peace of mind. You may want to speak up to put an end to how you're being treated. Cling to *that* reason in the moments you are tempted to shy away.

PHYSIOLOGY AS A FACTOR

There are also physiological responses that make the idea of speaking honestly with our friends completely terrifying. For those of us who get especially anxious with confrontation, our body will literally have its own triggered responses while we wonder, "Do I address this or let it go... again?"

Kristin Atchison, a psychology professor at Georgia State, points out another underlying factor that makes us avoid conflict and vulnerability, and it has to do with the anterior cingulate cortex— the part of our brain that controls empathy and decision-making.

"Tylenol can lessen social pain as well as physical pain," Professor Atchison says. "There is real pain associated with this. And across cultures, some cultures [even] describe social pain with the exact same words as they use for physical pain. They don't differentiate between them the way that we do in our language."

Atchison speaks to the neurological forces working to move us away from any semblance of suffering. Whether it is physical or emotional, our brain, according to her explanation, registers it the same way. Our inclination to run away from the discomfort and rejection that comes along with calling out our girlfriends (*Challenging* courage sector) or communicating our boundaries (*Preserving* courage sector) is only natural, because we know that the (culturally designed) ramifications would be too much to bear... despite mounting research that shows the benefits of speaking honestly.

YOUR BODY'S RESPONSE TO STRESS

Your breathing will quicken, and your palms get a little clammy. Your heart beats faster while your neck and throat tighten. All of these responses were once used to cue us that danger was near and to activate our "fight or flight" response.

What's even crazier is that "fight or flight" concept that you're so familiar with isn't all there is to the story. It turns out that when it was introduced in the early 1900s, mostly men were used for the study. When psychologist Shelley E. Taylor re-did the study about our responses to stress in 1998, she included more than 200 women. She found that we actually have more range than "fight or flight." For women, when put into situation where our adrenaline surges, we respond one of two ways: we either tend to or befriend?

TEND OR BEFRIEND

When faced with a stress-inducing situation, we may begin to TEND to their needs and work to protect them, ensuring that those in our circle are cared for. The other response we may have is to BEFRIEND. This is when we seek community and find someone to talk and commiserate with to work out our situation. While men may certainly have these responses, they are less likely to engage them the way we do. Our brains make oxytocin (the feel good hormone) when we are stressed and because of our estrogen, we use it as fuel to join with other women and override any fear or panic associated with the threat.

This is even more reason to build a circle of friends we really care for and that allows us to be ourselves. When we face the stresses of the outside world, we need a band of woman we feel compelled to protect and support. We also need a group that we can run to as we search for ways to survive harsh and unpredictable curveballs life throws our way. Tough-love friendships allow us a space where, no matter our instinct to tend or befriend, each of those physiological responses can thrive.

Daniel Golman, the author of "Emotional Intelligence," nicknamed this response as the Amygdala Hijack (because the amygdala is the part of your brain responsible for your emotions).

When your brain perceives a threat (*If I tell her this, she'll run away... If I share my full self with her, she'll misunderstand me... If I address her behavior, she'll ice me out of the group...*), it takes an immediate and overwhelming reaction that's often disproportionate to the actual risk.

The way our brains are designed, the situation ("stimuli") hits our thalamus, which sends a message to our amygdala (the part that manages emotion) *before* it even hits our neocortex to process and reason.

What does this look like in action?

Your girlfriend says something super insensitive. Again. She means no harm, but it sends a jolt through your body every time. As soon as it happens, you'll either begin to get anxious as your work to withhold your discomfort and opinions inside (an absence of tough love that confronts— lovingly) or respond right away by telling her how it wasn't cool and unloading on her (the absence of tough love that confronts— longingly). Our brains literally take over in the moments of conflict with our friends, and our decision to exercise tough love or not (vulnerable but firm "truth-tellings" delivered with compassion) and we have physiological responses as we work to determine what to do.

But do you have the kind of relationship that allows you to confidently present your diverging opinions? Think back to the four courage sectors (outlined in chapter 2). Are you able to freely *Share* (be vulnerable), *Preserve* (set boundaries), *Affirm* (encourage) and *Challenge* (hold her accountable)? Do you two have intimacy in your friendship, which allows you to stay emotionally connected despite differing needs, beliefs, and personalities? Are you safe to express how you really feel?

ANXIOUS, MUCH?

There is so much within our control, but it's funny to see how our brains can place (navigable) obstacles to operating authentically in our friendships. But it's a matter of being aware of our design.

Remember, while we are wired to be empathetic (a beautiful thing!), we can't allow ourselves to be so concerned with making others uncomfortable that we sacrifice our own well being.

And while some of us opt to "run away" in the face of danger, we don't have to be passive when conflict or disagreement happens with our friends. We also don't have to focus on taking care of others (TEND) or gather support to handle something head-on (BEFRIEND). By re-framing the way we see conflict, we can seize more opportunities to courageously and independently initiate moments that will ultimately bring us more peace and understanding in our friendships.

If you generally have anxiety, the thought of (lovingly) confronting a friend about something will inevitably stir feelings of nervousness. But here are specific tips for my anxious ladies that you can follow before having the conversation:

1. <u>Say "no" to coffee— and dessert</u>. Okay, this is where you're tempted to cut me off, but her me out. The caffeine in coffee in the sugar in sweets, despite being our familiar go-to stress-relievers— actually wire us and make anxious people more anxious. If you plan to chat with your friend about something that's concerning you, it would be in your best interest to avoid eating these things before or during the conversation.

2. <u>Remember to breathe</u>. Seriously. This is advice I've given to female students when came to me worked up about a presentation they were about to give; to PR clients before they did a television interview; and to coaching clients when they nervously introduce a vulnerable topic. And it sounds so freaking, insulting, doesn't it? When people suggest you breathe, the remarkably simple suggestion seems ineffective at quelling very big, very real fears.

But dang, man,—it works.

As soon as you begin taking intentionally deep breaths, it sends a message to a pocket of neurons in your brain that control feelings of stress. Do it when you're getting worked up about the idea of expressing yourself truthfully to your friends. Counteract rapid, anxious breaths that may "talk you out of" speaking your mind.

3. <u>Acknowledge your anxiety instead of pretending you don't feel nervous</u>. One of the most common pieces of advice that counselors give to people with

anxiety is to look it in the face. There's something about saying, "Man, I feel anxious about this" that deflates your nervous energy. Spiraling completely cripples us, yanking us down a path of ominous *"what if's"*- *"What if I bring this up to her and she totally hates me? What if she tells the other girls and they ice me out? What if I start turning red or stuttering while I'm talking to her? Maybe this is my problem and not hers. Yeah, that's it. This is going to completely ruin me."*

Also try to remember what will happen if you choose to remain silent: A. There are physical effects of unexpressed anger and/ or frustration which include increased blood pressure, poor sleep, tense muscles and migraines. Keeping your concerns inside *will not make your issues go away*, because your feelings are going to manifest themselves somehow and B. There are psychological effects of unverbalized stress that are no joke. Holding back literally plays with your mind. You may find yourself beginning to feel lonely (as the internal thoughts begin to overwhelm you, causing you to feel isolated from others), and you can become depressed. This affects your sleep too, and can lead to a litany of other physical and mental issues.

Not to dramatize this point too much, but working to avoid confrontation is you saying that you'd rather physically suffer than deal with tough issues head on (which may be stressful, yes, but the awkwardness is temporary).

It's wild to think that there are neurological and physiological influences in our everyday dealings with our friends. But as you become more aware of what's working in the background and how it may be helping or hindering your approach to conflict, you'll be one step closer to exercising more courage in your relationships with other women.

When It's All in Your Head

Although our society, fundamental human needs, and brain design all influence our ability and willingness to be honest in our friendships, much of our reluctance can be traced back to our own self-induced fears.

One of the primary reasons we don't develop tough-love friendships is because confrontation itself makes us generally uncomfortable. We'll justify our avoidance with reasoning like: *I don't need to say anything because these things have a way of working themselves out. Everything will be fine!*

Ah, the "optimist."

Some of us have convinced ourselves that there's no need to voice our concerns because — with a little bit of time and a whole lot of hope— the situation will take care of itself. While this desire to "let fate work it out" comes from a noble place, it lets us off the hook. If there is a situation that is less than ideal, we have to call it out because remaining silent:

1. negatively impacts our mental, physical, and emotional well-being
2. enables our friends to stay in a behavior or mentality that could be unhealthy to themselves or to others
3. keeps our friendship from being as honest and intimate as it could be

Anxiety is a beast. Even those who don't regularly deal with anxiety may find themselves hesitant to travel into sensitive territory with a friend over delicate issues. Whenever you're dealing with matters of the heart, the terrain is fragile and often unpredictable. Approaching anything with this kind of importance requires caution.

But the fact that it's tricky can't be a reason not to have the conversation.

The trouble with avoiding confrontation is that it only offers a temporary reprieve from conflict. But it's a delusional fog, and while you may initially feel like you are avoiding problems by refusing to acknowledge them, the truth is, eventually the conflict will emerge anyway—and this time, uglier and messier than it would've been if you'd addressed it head-on.

ANXIOUS IN SILENCE, ANXIOUS IN SPEAKING

A story of two new moms makes this point more clearly.

I spoke with a woman named Gina about conflict she was having with a "mom friend," Marabella. Gina is a mom of two, working long hours as a nurse and spending her "off hours" as an involved and attentive mother. She's known Marabella for 4 years, connecting during a mommy group shortly after they each had their first child.

While the friendship grew out of a space of mutual struggles surviving new motherhood, they became each other's support systems, emotionally and physically, when the other was feeling particularly overwhelmed. They were fast friends, laughing during times of joy and commiserating during the particularly low points of motherhood.

They got pregnant again around the same time, and after Gina and Marabella each had a second child, the tone between them began to shift. Gina was trying to balance work, mothering, and marriage, while stay-at-home Marabella actually quickly adapted and thrived with her second child. This confidence translated into increased commentary to Gina, as she began remarking on Gina's mothering style and making suggestions to "help." Marabella addressed what she saw as Gina struggling, and gave advice liberally.

For nearly a year, Gina dealt with the shame-inciting comments. Marabella was quick to let Gina know that she was dressing her son inappropriately; that she should find a way to balance both the household chores and mothering so her husband "didn't have to do so much" of the domestic work; and that she was feeding her daughter solids too soon.

While Marabella's attitude could easily be read as judgmental by outsiders, the truth is that Marabella thought she had the freedom in the friendship to share her thoughts about Gina's choices and style. She genuinely saw it as guidance, nearly thinking it altruistic of herself to devote so much energy and attention to Gina's parenting.

But Marabella's intentions didn't matter. Gina was fuming inside. And for nearly a year, she withheld her growing rage.

Her friends had noticed. With every new offense, Gina called up other friends, reporting on Marabella's latest provocations and sharing her disbelief.

"I mean, *who* says that? Who tells another woman that she's dressing her kids wrong? She's ridiculous, right?" Gina vented almost daily to mutual friends who were familiar with Marabella's ways.

Her friends noticed her irritability and passive aggressive behavior. Whenever they talked about anything, Gina found a way to connect it back to her issue with Marabella, subjecting everyone to listen, once more, as she went on about how awful she was. The tension was festering inside of her, and quickly turned into bitterness.

But whenever friends encouraged Gina to share her frustrations with Marabella, Gina responded:

"Nah, I can't do that. Conflict makes me anxious."

Instead, she brainstormed ways to manage the issue that didn't involve addressing her Marabella directly:

I think I'm just gonna ignore her every time she says something crazy... Maybe whenever she gives me her opinion on how to do something with the girls I'll just say, 'Oh, well that's one way to look at it.'... Should I just stop inviting her over completely? I'm just going to avoid her for a while. I'm not gonna deal with that.

The problem was that not only did Gina refuse to address her issues directly with Marabella, but that she'd created entire false narratives of what could go wrong once she did. She allowed those assumptions about potential fallout to completely immobilize her.

Even her husband had grown weary of her complaints. But not one for conflict himself, he encouraged her to "just ignore it" and to "stop

making a big deal" of the issue.

Here's the kicker: When I asked Marabella about Gina, she spoke tenderly, explaining how she is doing all she can to help Gina manage. She showed an earnest concern about Gina's physical and mental health, and revealed that she tries to help by giving her advice whenever she sees Gina in a moment of difficulty. She describes their friendship as one of the best things in her life, clearly unaware of how Gina perceives the state of their relationship.

Sadly, Gina never found a way to directly address Marabella's behavior, and during a girls' night out, lost her cool over Marabella's comments about one of Gina's young daughters staying up too late. Gina exploded, unleashing a year's worth of resentment in one 30-minute tirade. Marabella, of course, felt completely blindsided by the outburst, because her narrative of the last year was completely different, which put her in the position of a woman wrongfully accused.

Tensions were high between both families for months afterwards, and awkwardness abounded as their children's birthday parties came and went. But after seeing each other at enough mutual friends' events and gradually speaking again, they finally had a conversation about the misunderstanding, with Gina expressing her feelings of inadequacy and judgement in Marabella's presence, and Marabella explaining her commentary as her way of demonstrating her love for Gina and her children.

"Tough-love friendship" gives freedom for both women involved. For the one who initiates hard conversations, she'll find herself liberated from her silent internal conflict and tension. The friend who is invited into the conversation will be free of her one-sided narrative, gaining a full understanding of the picture in front of her. And, if handled with the proper compassion and humility, their friendship can enter a new level of trust and appreciation.

WHEN GETTING IN YOUR HEAD GETS IN YOUR WAY

But withholding our feelings, needs, and desires from our friends only creates distance and resentment. Many times, the suppressing comes from within, a decision we impose on ourselves.

Many therapists will tell you that fear of confrontation is a common catalyst for anxiety "episodes." Sometimes, we'll justify our avoidance by saying we don't want to "rock the boat," but the fact is that telling our truth is only going to result in more depth in our relationships— not less.

Most people are so busy working to avoid present pain that they overlook the long-term peace and resolution that lies at the end of an honest conversation.

Here's what can be done for those who get "in their heads" about speaking directly with a friend:

1. *Stop the mental hypotheticals for what "could go wrong."* Oftentimes, those who avoid conflict do so because they've dreamed up 100 scenarios of what could go wrong if they actually have a tough conversation. Ironically, we do this with our female friends and feel justified in doing so because we think our "knowing" them makes our dreamed-up scenarios more likely. But whether we know someone or not, we can never predict outcomes. The only way we will know how things will turn out it to pursue resolution. This is especially important because many find that direct addressing often leads to positive outcomes, with the other person becoming a willing participant in wanting harmony.

2. *Re-think the way you see confrontation.* If you associate honest and direct conversation with negativity, then of course you'll work to avoid it at all costs. But if you reframe your thinking and view tough love conversations, instead, as the very means to finding understanding, it won't be something you run from; it will be the very thing you run to.

3. *Take baby steps.* One overwhelming aspect of confrontation is the weight of addressing a heavy topic. But what if the conversation didn't have to be so all-encompassing? Instead of sitting your friend down to talk formally, why not first just respond the next time she says something offensive and only comment on the issue at hand? Try not to feel the need to approach the larger, full-scale issue you have with a friend. Test the waters by beginning with the smaller issue before approaching the more holistic subject.

FEELING UNQUALIFIED TO SPEAK UP

Anxiety is not the only personal factor that gets in the way of us confronting our friends.

Another reason we shy away from tough conversations is because we feel unqualified, thinking: **I don't have my *own* stuff together, so how can I confront her about her stuff?**

Sometimes the topics we want to address involve her own shortcomings and (unbeknownst to us) insecurities. Knowing this, we grow sensitive to the idea of touching on those areas, feeling unqualified in the midst of our own shortcomings and insecurities.

In my opinion, this attitude stems from imposter syndrome, a psychological phenomenon that involves feeling unequipped and unworthy of your position and achievements

Once we've entered into a space of trusted friendship, we are automatically placed into the position of confidant and partner. One role of a true friend is to help another see areas where she could be experiencing more fullness in her life. We have the privilege to be trusted as her "challenger," a role that allows us to push back—with compassion.

But our minds trick us into thinking we're not fit to say anything— despite our friends' love for us, and despite the friendship's need for honesty— and we talk ourselves out of having very necessary conversations. We allow our focus to be on our own issues to invalidate the healthy insight we may have for others.

We think *Who am I to say anything? I'm not perfect myself.*

If you have taken the time to observe, and there is something happening that doesn't sit well with your spirit or that you can help shine light on, then your opinion *is* valid. Your concerns *are* valid. Your remarks *are* valid. Especially if you have taken the time to ask God for guidance (what to share with your friend and how to say it, asking "Lord, what should I do here?"), and truly feel prompted to speak, then you should. But despite the nagging pull, we talk ourselves out of confronting our friends by discounting our own authority as her confidant.

And consider for a moment, if you thought about "having your stuff together" before approaching your friend about hers. What if that were actually the rule? For the most part, on most subjects, none of us would be saying a word! We wouldn't be having any conversations at all! When you consider that we're all progressing and growing a little more each day, none of us is in a space to speak to our girlfriends as life experts.

I can't stress this enough: "Tough love" is not synonymous with "criticizing." Criticism is telling your friend you disapprove of one of her faults. Tough love is inviting her to a conversation to understand why she's doing what she's doing, and then challenging her by offering a new perspective so she can operate at higher standard for herself, for you, and for your friendship.

If you're struggling with feeling qualified to speak to your friends about hard things, consider this: There is actually power in your "insufficiency." The irony is that your lack of qualification totally qualifies you. Remember, you are not her counselor or adviser or therapist. You're her friend. And sometimes it's easier to receive a call-out from someone who's open about their own faults because you know they're coming from a humble, helpful space. You know they want to come alongside you to offer both community and accountability.

WALKING BESIDE HER

If I can tell a friend that I too have experienced (or am experiencing) self-destructive behaviors after a break-up, then she may be more inclined to listen because I am presenting myself as a peer who is willing to come alongside her — not in front of her, but with her arm-in-arm, step-by-step. This is better than someone walking in front of her, shaming her with an, 'I overcame this so why can't you?" attitude.

Or worse, an attitude that says, "I never struggled with this particular thing so how could you be struggling with it?" Our struggles and hurdles are different, but we're all out here trying to figure it out. Approaching her by using your own inadequacies to level the playing field makes your message a bit more palatable. In the next chapter, you'll learn a helpful acronym as a framework for approaching tough conversations.

One of our most underutilized tools is our vulnerability. It sounds counterintuitive, but if you've ever let your guard down and found community in the process, then you know I'm telling the truth. By letting her know it's something you are working on too, she may be more receptive, because you're now entering the conversation as a partner instead of as an accomplished adviser.

This approach also tends to prevent her from thinking you're being judgmental, as she'll find assurance in your genuine intentions. By sharing that you've had the same struggle, you may motivate her to want to do the work because it is something that you'll will go through together.

That thought is also coming from the expectation that the "tough-love truth-teller" teller has to provide answers. But you can take a deep breath in knowing this: Having all the answers is not your job.

When we enter into a hard conversation with a friend, we don't have to come prepared with a plan to show her the way out of her issues. It wouldn't be a peer-to-peer conversation if we did. Sometimes it's about figuring it out together, a fair and open dialogue about the matter at hand. Our only job is to have the courage to lovingly present it and then hold her hand (should she take it) as you both navigate the issue together. Even when we are equipped with suggestions for solutions they do not come from a place of expertise.

If the ultimate goal is to experience more depth with the women in our lives, we have to find a way to let our guards down, which means finding a way to initiate tough conversations with the people we love most.

Tough Love: How to Give It

Hard words, if they be true, are better than soft words, if they be false.
Charles Spurgeon

As a new college freshman, I immediately enrolled in the two courses I didn't have a chance to take in high school: Human Sexuality and Speech 101.

While my high school offered speech courses, the elective never aligned with my schedule. And as for the Human Sexuality course? I'd taken health classes in high school, but they were bland fact-sessions about reproduction. I wanted the Human Sexuality class not because I was necessarily interested in anatomy, but because— well, I was a curious virgin and the course title alone was enough to make me blush.

I got more than I bargained for in both classes.

The sexuality class was taught by an 80-year-old woman who was wildly unafraid to call body parts by their rightful names. It was awesome, but it left my inexperienced brain with more questions than answers.

The speech class surprised me, too. It was about more than stringing words together and walking around stage like a rock star. I thought it would be all about me, and having been told "You should be a speaker!" before (mostly because I talk a lot, less because people thought I was insightful), I was excited at the idea of being the star of the show for a full semester.

I originally enrolled in the course because I wanted to talk… and I wanted people to have to listen to me.

But the "Speech 101" curriculum centered around the "non-shiny" things I hadn't considered: the importance of nonverbal cues, thought organization, research and reasoning, and ironically... listening.

That speech class was nothing I'd anticipated but everything I needed. It changed me so much, as it got me to thinking about why the class wasn't required for every human being on the planet.

In 15 weeks, I'd learned how to stop focusing on myself, and instead, plug into others around me. I learned that the message doesn't matter if it's not delivered the right way, and your audience determines the success of your speech. The class was "others-focused," bringing me face-to-face with my lack of thoughtfulness. When the class was over, I found myself applying the lessons to nearly every interaction thereafter.

IN NEED OF A SKILL

I have watched with both familiarity and wonder every time conflict arises between women. I watched it play out for seven years between high school girls in the hallways. I hear it as my female PR clients unintentionally confess their secret frustrations and fears during our prep meetings. I hear it when my coaching clients share their desires to tell their friends an honest truth, but are immobilized by a host of fears and concerns.

It's everywhere: my Bible study groups, book clubs, women's networking circles. From teenage girls to top female executives— we struggle with an internal fury to tell other women how we really feel. But we are captive to society's norms, social conditioning, and our own insecurities.

When it comes to showing "tough love" and having hard conversations, women either deal with it head-on or avoid it altogether. But oftentimes, the women who jump in and "tell it like it is" are often doing it wrong. And the women who run away from the confrontation? Well, they're actually dying to express themselves, fantasizing about what would happen if they just went for it. But they don't have the courage, and even if they did, they don't feel equipped.

This is something I have informally observed hundreds of times, wondering if I was the only one who noticed. So I conducted an online survey to discover if what I was witnessing wasn't just in my head.

Spoiler alert: I'm not imagining things.

64% of respondents admitted they'd like to finally have a hard heart-to-heart with a girlfriend, but just didn't know where to start.

While there are several factors that determine whether or not we engage in tough conversations, one of them shouldn't be because we simply don't know how.

We need something to help us through, so I created a framework based on ten years of informal observation and six years of formal communications experience. The purpose of the framework is to outline the six critical factors and considerations when approaching a difficult conversation with a female friend. While there are other communication strategies and outlines, I have not seen one built specifically for the nuance of platonic woman-to-woman relationships. The framework I created accounts for this unique dynamic.

S.E.T. THE MI.C.: A FRAMEWORK

There are other communication frameworks and strategies that exist, of course, but in the years that I've studied communication, I have yet to see one designed to account for our sensitivities and strengths (like, for example, the way that we're so good at reading subtext).

The framework is built on an acronym: S.E.T the M.I.C.

When I was in college, I had a band. When we arrived before shows to begin setting up, we'd load our equipment onto the stage and start with a mic check to make sure that all the levels were set. We called it "setting the mics" as we tested the drums, saxophone, piano, guitar, vocals— they all had to be "mic'd up" in a way where they would both be heard individually but also blend with the other instruments. If the microphone near the saxophone was too loud, for example, the audience would notice and it would distract from the overall song. *It would affect their entire listening experience.*

The same is true of delivering a tough-love truth-telling.

If you fail to "set the mic" before inviting a friend into a sensitive yet necessary "keep it real" conversation, you may be setting yourself up to be misheard. You've got to have the right attitude in place before you can begin to speak your truth. If you don't, it *could affect her entire listening experience.*

Allow the acronym "S.E.T. the M.I.C." to serve as helpful reminder of all the elements that need to be in place before you confront your girlfriends. If just one of these is absent, it can significantly shift the outcome.

Before you even begin the conversation, your mentality must be that of curiosity, not judgment. If you're entering to tell before you question, then you may want to rethink your approach. While you may certainly need to courageously communicate your message, the conversation should be more of a dialogue in which you are working to better understand your *friend*, not forcing her better understand *you*.

A FRAMEWORK FOR DIFFICULT CONVERSATIONS

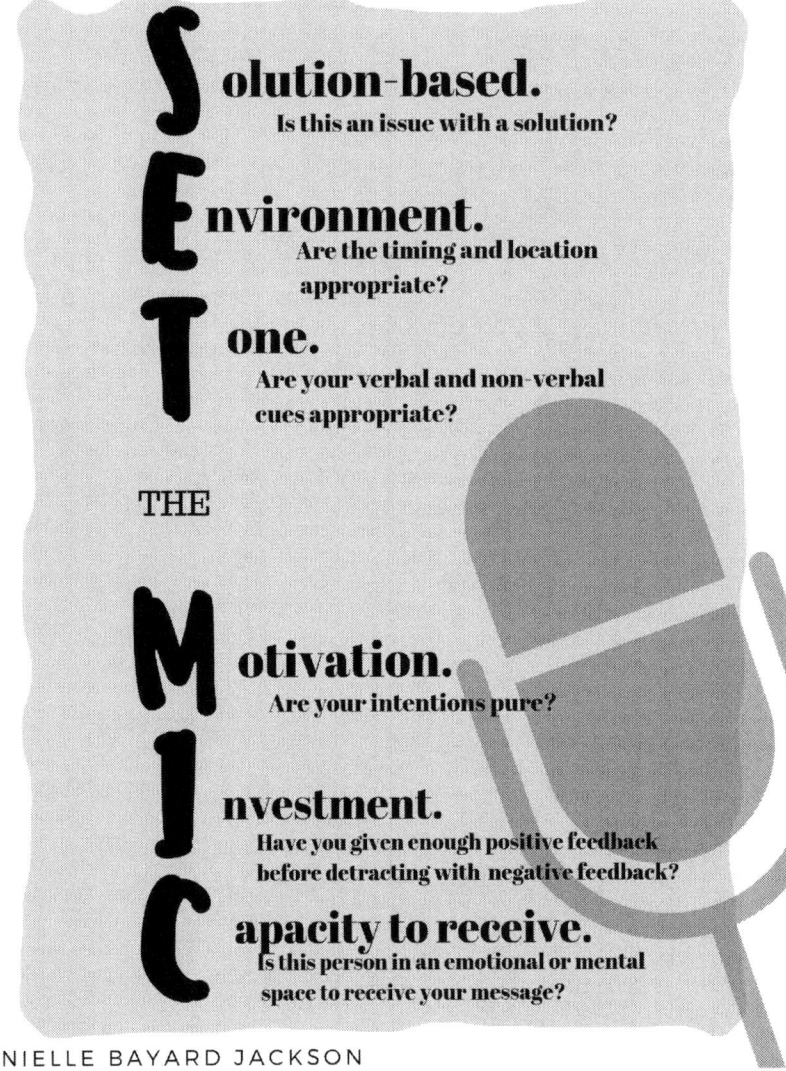

Solution-based. Is this an issue with a solution?

Environment. Are the timing and location appropriate?

Tone. Are your verbal and non-verbal cues appropriate?

THE

Motivation. Are your intentions pure?

Investment. Have you given enough positive feedback before detracting with negative feedback?

Capacity to receive. Is this person in an emotional or mental space to receive your message?

DANIELLE BAYARD JACKSON

The S.E.T. the M.I.C. acronym stands for:

SOLUTION-BASED

Before you invite your girlfriend into a tough-love heart-to-heart, you must first ask yourself if you can identify a problem that has an actual solution. If your complaint or concern is about something that is not within her power to change, then don't even consider talking to her about it. Remember, the purpose of a hard conversation is to share your truth while also gaining a better understanding of hers. But if you're exploring an issue that can't be solved, it can quickly become a tell-off session or an argument that goes in circles.

Sharing that you're concerned her negative mindset is holding her back? She can change that. You can help. Telling her that she continues to cross one of your personal boundaries? She can change that. You can help. Inviting her into a conversation about how her self-degradation undercuts her beauty? She can change that. You can help.

ENVIRONMENT

Although we typically think of a physical location when we think of environment, we often forget that it includes both the conditions of our surroundings and our timing.

Be sure to only enter into a tough-love conversation if you are in a space with few interruptions. For example, if you are chatting in your house, that could work because it's safe and familiar. But if you also have your two-year-old running around, the environment won't be conducive to diving into sensitive territory because it's difficult to think and speak freely between toddler squeals and the sound of a child running around. Inviting someone into a space of reflection and compassionate discussion is already unpredictable terrain. The goal is to minimize surprises that could detract from your focus when you're trying to meaningfully engage.

Timing is also an element of the environment, because it plays a role in the overall space you'll be in. Speaking to a girlfriend in a physical or emotional time that's not set up for her (or you) to bring her best self could be problematic.

If your true goal is to have corrected behavior or improved relationship, then you have to deliver your message at the right time. Your friend's just been dumped by her boyfriend? Not the ideal time to tell her it's her fault for remaining in that relationship longer than she should've. Co-worker walking out of a presentation she totally bombed? Not the best time to tell her she could've avoided the disaster if she'd just been better prepared.

This is challenging because, if you're anything like me, we are moved by our emotions. And it's difficult to withhold what you want to say at the time you feel moved to say it. But our impulses can get us into trouble if they're not tapered by patience and thoughtfulness.

Remember: If the goal is to help her, help your friendship, or spur some kind of positive change, then the last thing you want to do is turn her off because you simply couldn't wait.

If you're struggling to guess when the right time is, I highly encourage you to start by asking her straight out: *"Hey Tanya, can I talk to you about something?"* or *"Girl, I've had something on my heart I wanted to talk to you about. When is a good time to really work through some of that?"* or *"Okay, can I offer you some feedback on something that's been on my mind?"* or *"I wanted to ask you more about something you said the other day, but I want to dig in when we're not so distracted. When's a good time for you?"* Sometimes it's better to ask if she wants to hear it, or find out if she's emotionally available to hear it—you don't always have to have hard-truth conversations unsolicited.

While on the surface this could just look like the dreaded "We need to talk," it's different because it invites her to set the time, and it tells her upfront that you've got something on your mind. It should never be used in a way to intentionally build suspense or cause drama. The goal should be to actually ease any impending tension and to enter into the conversation on an even playing field.

Exercise thoughtfulness in identifying the optimal time to go all in with friend, because although tough love hinges on truth-telling, it becomes cruel if it's given at the wrong time. In our eagerness to cut the crap and give our friends unfiltered honesty, we risk coming across as insensitive if we blindside them with hard-hitting truths smack in the middle of times they are most vulnerable. Being in a position of (perceived) failure and insecurity is already such a tender space. We are open and raw and completely exposed. It's possible that this is how your girlfriend will feel once you pull her aside. And if she makes the *brave* choice of being vulnerable with you only to have you hit her while she feels weak, it can *feel* like a betrayal.

Now trust me, I'm not saying that every truth bomb be cushioned in bubble wrap and delivered over wine between hesitant apologies. I'm just saying that we may completely get in the way of our objective (helping our friend heal) if we hit her when she is most exposed. Do it privately (never publicly) and when your friend is not irritated, so your message is well received.

And don't just consider timing for her. Think about yourself. If you are ticked about something she's said or if you haven't taken the time to really process why you want to show a little tough love, then you shouldn't be doing it. Take the time to collect your thoughts and check in with your own emotions.

TONE

When discussing tone, typically we're referring to the volume and intensity of someone's voice. We think of whether someone's speaking earnestly or sarcastically, condescendingly or humbly. It goes without saying that having a compassionate tone is ideal for a conversation where you're exploring some pretty difficult truths.

But the nonverbal messages you're sending contribute just as much— actually, more— to the conversation.

Working in public relations brings me all kinds of cool opportunities. At my agency, we work on fun campaigns with objectives to increase sales, brand awareness, and overall visibility. It's the fun side of reputation management.

But the reality is that we sometimes have to deal with the not-so-pleasant side of PR: crisis management. When we prepare clients to publicly address a sensitive subject, we go beyond creating talking points. Let's be honest: it doesn't matter if a client reads a statement about how sorry she is if she is stiff, or rolling her eyes... or avoiding eye contact altogether. Her body language can't contradict her message.

The things we don't say often matter more than what we do.

This advice applies to more than public relations. It's one of the single most important social skills. And it's an area where women really excel.

READING THE SUBTEXT: A GIFT AND A CURSE

Research shows that women are actually better than men at decoding nonverbal cues. Judith A. Hall, a social psychologist, conducted more than 70 extensive studies to determine which gender displayed a greater ability to read body language and other messages sent without using words. She found that, despite the age being tested, females show a greater ability to assess things like body language, micro-expressions (the small facial expressions we make but try to hide), and auditory cues like inflection and tone.

The upside to this is that we can walk away from a conversation with more information than a man would. We are so in tune with all that's *not* being said! But this can be tricky when having a heart-to-heart with another woman. Our ability to read nonverbal cues and subtext can lead to a loaded conversation where we both walk away working to make sense of what was shared (and all that wasn't). Oftentimes, we won't even address the inflection change in her voice or the way her body shifts, and we'll just "read," store it, and process it along with what she says.

When it comes to intentionally or unintentionally delivering nonverbal cues (eye rolls, change from fast-talking to slow-talking, raised eyebrows, and shifts in posture), you want to be aware of how you're coming across. Is your body language getting in the way of the message you're trying to convey?

We must also be mindful of over-reading nonverbal cues and subtext from other women. Most times, they're great indicators of how she really feels, and these cues provide necessary information as we work to process her message. But it can also work to our detriment if we place subtext where there isn't any.

My husband took me to see Trevor Noah when he visited our city on his comedy tour. One of the jokes Trevor made was about how men and women can walk away from the same conversation and have two very different interpretations.

"Guys, if you both pass one of her old co-workers on the street, they'll both say 'hello.' 'Hey girl, how are you?' 'I'm good girl, how are you?' 'Good! It's nice to see you.' 'Yeah, you too!' 'Okay, bye.' 'Bye.'"

"When you walk away, you'll probably say something like, 'Wow, she seems nice.' But be careful because you know your girl's gonna say, ' Are you kidding? Did you see how rude she was just now?'"

Of course the joke was received with roaring laughter and applause, and I was especially entertained. Perhaps the reason it was so funny to all of us was because it was so freaking true. But there's truth to every joke. With such a strong radar for nonverbal cues, we've got to be mindful of how we deliver and interpret them when we're entering into a tough love conversation with a friend.

MOTIVATION AND INTENTION

What is done in love is done well. —Vincent van Gogh

Examine your intentions before you invite your friend into a sensitive conversation. What do you really want out of this? What would be your ideal outcome? What reaction are you looking for?

Others may disagree, but I believe if there is any part of you that takes pleasure in giving a hard truth that could be hurtful to your friends, you need to re-examine your friendship. By nature, tough love gently and courageously confronts tough subjects in the hope of sparking productive change. It's hard because it is unpleasant, but it's so necessary.

Sometimes dishing out tough love can be a relief because it's often the first step toward *better*. But it's hard to do because we are naturally so protective over those we love. Yet if there is any feeling of "Let me tell this chick about herself," then do not call it tough love. That's something else entirely: self-righteousness.

We also have to be sure that our goal is not to incite shame. If we are trying to motivate by provoking guilt or shame, we have already missed the mark. Tough love is not an excuse to impulsively dish out harsh criticism, masking reckless remarks as an attempt to be helpful.

INTIMACY AND INVESTMENT

Before initiating a tough conversation with a friend, you need to seriously measure your investment and commitment to the relationship. This includes your dedication to her in the past and present.

Concerning the past, ask yourself, "Do I give more negative feedback than positive?" This matters when you are considering offering a message that could be perceived as negative. In fact, there was a study done in the 1970s that tracked the happiness level of couples over a period of nine years. The study revealed that the couples who offered 5 positive for every 1 negative transaction had a greater sense of satisfaction in their romantic relationship.

Friendships are no different here. If every opinion you offer to your friend is negative, then you haven't "invested" enough positive feedback to make that "withdrawal." No matter how valid your "constructive" comment may be, it may be hard to receive if you never give voice to the positive things in your friendship, or about your friend specifically. If you are not pouring encouragement into her life (the AFFIRMING sector of the Tough-Love Friendship Model), then it's not fair to liberally give your negative remarks.

Measure your message against the time you've invested in the friendship before determining whether or not it's appropriate to invite her into a hard conversation.

CAPACITY TO RECEIVE

The last factor you should consider before having a hard talk is her capacity to receive the message you're trying to deliver. If she is in a place in her life that is especially defensive or distorted, would she be in a state of mind to accept or appreciate your honesty?

Does she have the emotional awareness to engage with you? Give thought to the season she may be in, the level of sensitivity and insecurity surrounding the matter, and what she has to lose if you invite her into the conversation.

This does not mean that if you anticipate your friend's discomfort, you should avoid the conversation. This points, however, to a certain level of instability or emotional immaturity that would make the conversation unproductive from the very beginning.

SINKING THE BOAT

Giving a "tough-love truth-telling" requires courage because not only must you okay with *rocking* the boat, you have to be okay with the possibility of sinking the whole damn thing.

Ideally you'd invite your friend into a conversation about the fractures she's causing in your friendship, she would concede and admit that her actions are detrimental, she'd thank you for bringing it to her attention, and you two would instantly be closer than ever.

In reality, it's likely that there will be tears and defenses, misunderstandings, and distance. There may be temporary tension while everyone remains on guard: she of her heart, you of your intentions. You'll have to clarify what you meant, she'll look for subtext in your words. Why? Because conflict is messy and unpredictable, despite our best effort and intention. We can come to the table with a carefully prepared script, while remaining completely unaware the other person is arriving with a full-powered shredder, ready to rip our rehearsed monologue to pieces.

And when that happens, *then what?* Are you mentally and emotionally prepared for the dialogue to take a life of its own and lead you both down a path you weren't expecting?

When I coached my students, I noticed that much of their frustration was not with the course or the content— it was with unmet expectations. And I've found this to be the case in most things I've pursued: marriage, motherhood… hell, season 2 of *This is Us*. Intellectually, we know that you can rarely manage or predict outcomes of the situations you enter into, but the way we fall apart and become discouraged says otherwise.

Typically when we go into a hard conversation with an image of how things will go, we subconsciously work to move things in a pre-determined direction. Our comments and questions are more pointed; if she responds with a comment that's "off-script," we pull her back onto the course we prepared; we are silently directing instead of allowing her to play the role of her choosing.

Three ways to manage your expectations of a tough conversation:
1. View the "truth-telling" as an equal exchange instead of a one-sided vent session.
2. Enter the conversation with a sense of wonder.
3. Use more questions than statements during the conversation.

"Call-outs" are inevitable in any *real* friendship. As long as you've packaged it fairly and respectfully, she should be reminded during the exchange that you care for her and have her best interest in mind. It may not be resolved right away. If there is gray area after your conversation for a while ("Are we still cool? Are we going to be okay?") that's fine. It's expected. Don't fight it. Let the process do its work.

Quick tips for a successful tough-love conversation:
- Take turns
- Respect her position
- Ask questions
- No blaming, shaming
- Avoid alcohol

- Stick to one issue, attack situation not judgement
- Explain how it affects friendship or concern for her
- Try not to include third parties
- Humor is okay if not ridiculing
- Balance negative with positive (ideally, the 5:1 "magic ratio" mentioned earlier)

LEADING WITH VULNERABILITY

One suggestion I often give to those unsure of how to approach a difficult conversation is to lead with vulnerability.

One of the great barriers to good communication is the way we work so hard to find words that mask our true feelings. I speak like I'm tough to mask that I'm scared. We tell guys we're interested in that we don't care about something even though we really do. We tell our girlfriend that it's "totally cool" that she flaked for the third time even though we're disappointed and frustrated with her unreliability.

But the best thing to do is actual the most radical: say exactly what we mean.

Before you engage in a "tough love" conversation, you need to first identify *why* you are doing it *and* the reason you're anxious about having it. Then you need to put words to your concerns and use that as your opener.

Why?

Because it completely disarms her. In a world where "We need to talk" really means "There is something wrong and I want you to sit and listen as I list all the ways you need to fix the problem," we have been conditioned to come to the table with our emotional guard, ready to defend ourselves. But when we invite our girlfriend to the conversation by exposing our own weakness, we lessen her resistance by bringing a soft and human element to the table.

Are you nervous that by telling it like it is, she's going to cut you out? Tell her.

Are you worried that calling her out on her BS is going to make her badmouth you to the other women in your group? Say that.

Are you hesitant to have the conversation because you're worried she may misunderstand you? Say so.

It's a radical notion: confronting someone by first acknowledging your own insecurities. But it works. As we explored earlier chapters, there are several reasons why you're feeling nervous about confronting a friend, and it may be best if you start by telling her that.

I've been thinking about what to say to you for a while now, but I've been nervous to bring it up because I don't want to make you uncomfortable or create distance between us.

Girl, there have been some things happening lately that don't sit right with me, and I really want to talk about them but I don't want it to be something that gets out to the other ladies and causes unnecessary drama.

"WEAK SPEAK"

Once you've found the courage for a hard conversation, make sure your message isn't lost in a sea of weak language.

There is nothing worse than listening to someone who is muddling their message through a series of "Um's" and "I mean, I'm sorry" or "What I meant to say was…" We fall into what I call "weak speak" when we haven't thought through what we want to say, are unsure of ourselves, feel we have no right to express our truth, or are overly concerned with how we're being perceived.

The tell-tale signs of an unsure woman during tough conversation:

1. Backpedaling: Saying something, then taking it back.
2. Apologies: Softening otherwise "direct" statements with "I'm sorry's,"
3. Fillers: A series of "um's," "likes," and long pauses to fill the space where she hasn't thought her message through.
4. Self-deprecation: Making fun of ourselves to take the sting out of what she has to say. "I mean, that's how I feel but I can be a crybaby sometimes, so what do I know."

You will not hear this language from a woman who knows what she wants and is ready to go after real change in her friendships. So take the time to figure it out. How can you articulate very clearly and confidently your goal for the conversation if you haven't even thought it through?

INVITATION to DIALOGUE

It doesn't matter if you have known this girl for ten years—your perspective will always be limited. Despite the number of years you've observed certain behavior, despite how objectively you may BELIEVE you're seeing the situation, the truth is that you are still only seeing it from your limited perspective.

This means that your assessment of what's going on with her (she's too negative, her boyfriend is a total downgrade, she cares too much about what others think of her, she's grown selfish in the friendship lately) will still be subject to the little you see of the full picture.

For this reason, it's important that your conversation with her is an invitation to understanding. Though you'll come prepared with your intention and concerns, it should ultimately be a dialogue that leads you both to a place of better understanding.

Pose as many inviting statements as you can:

"Am I totally off base?" "I really want your help in understanding why things have been the way they've been lately... What am I missing?" "I want to have a better understanding of where you're coming from, but I need you to communicate with me..."

This is a key component in your truth-telling because it shows you value her voice. It shows humility as you admit you don't have the answers and need her help. It shows that you care about her as a person because your intention is to *understand*, not condemn.

If we keep in mind that tough-love friendship rests on doing hard things for the sake of greater intimacy and understanding—that closeness and acceptance are the end goal—then we set ourselves up for richer interactions with each other, no matter how difficult.

Tough Love: How to Take It

We were on the phone chatting about my 6-month-old son Elijah and a recent picture I'd posted on Facebook. Andrea was commenting on how big he'd gotten and I, in turn, made the usual jokes about how carrying him around was giving me Michelle Obama biceps.

After a few more minutes of playing catch-up, the conversation headed toward another social media post: a woman who'd attended my most recent public relations workshop shared a picture of me leading the training, and her caption mentioned something about learning a lot during the session.

Andrea's pace slowed, and she suddenly sounded very cautious.

"So, I see you were wearing jeans in the picture…"

Thinking it was a set-up to a joke, I laughed and confirmed the obvious. "Yeah… Why?"

"Well," she searched for the right words, "It's just that you're wearin' jeans to a lot of your events recently…really, since Elijah was born. It's good that you're getting out and about now, but… I mean, remember when you were like, stylin', girl?"

For the first few seconds, I was sure I didn't hear her correctly.

I leaned in hesitantly, trying my best to give her the benefit of the doubt by allowing more time to explain herself. Surely there was more. Surely I'd misunderstood.

"I mean, you know you look nice and professional in whatever you wear—always!" Andrea continued. "But I just… I know that since the baby… I know you were saying that it gets hectic at home sometimes and you don't have the time to do the things you used to. And you were telling me that you don't feel like yourself again yet and.. so I'm just saying… that maybe getting dressed up again will make you feel like yourself. I mean, you want your clients to take you seriously, right?"

I grabbed my emotional armor, jumping right into defender mode.

"Okaaaaaaay, well, my clients do take me seriously. Trust me. I don't think people are thinking that I don't know what I'm talking about just because I'm wearing jeans. Are you serious?"

I kept going. She'd hit a sore spot.

"And you know what? It's not like I walk in looking like a total bum! I mean, I style it up, you know? I'm just going for a relaxed style right now. I actually prefer it… And saying I won't be taken seriously? Trust me— trust me, no one's lookin' at me sideways because I'm wearing pants."

"Okay! I just—" Andrea tried to interject.

But once the defenses were out and once I'd been embarrassed, there was no stopping me. With each new point, my voice grew louder — my defenses stronger.

"I mean, if someone's judging me for wearing jeans and not for my experience, then—"

"Danielle!" Andrea cut in strong, working to clarify what she'd said. It was tense.

"I'm sorry. Of course people take you seriously," she apologized. I guess I'm just saying— you told me that you miss your old self, and I just thought that maybe this is one of those things. The baggy shirts, the jeans— I just thought that was a part of what you were talking about! I'm trying to encourage you. God, maybe I'm doing it wrong, I'm just trying to say I know you'd probably feel like your "best self" if you took the time to dress up like you used to. That's all."

I could hear the sincerity in her voice. Andrea was trying to communicate a hard truth to me and was doing her best to avoid landmines. As soon as I realized that she was actually trying to help, my defenses crumbled.

She was right.

This was not a shallow friend telling me to upgrade my wardrobe. This was a friend I'd had for years, finally calling me out on something I already knew to be true:

Since the baby, I'd put more of my energy into nurturing him and less on grooming myself. Because of the way my body changed and my hair had thinned after pregnancy, tending to myself felt both useless and incredibly painful— a reminder of how my appearance wasn't what I'd like it to be. Because I was in such a funk, I'd resorted to wearing the same pair of jeans… everywhere. I also began reaching for blouses that drowned me and I'd tuck them into my jeans, strategically masking spit-up and/ or breast milk stains.

I wish I was kidding.

My hair was often a little disheveled (in the kind of way that made you wonder if a gust of wind had JUST hit me before I'd walked in the room and I didn't notice), my shoes were often scuffed (because I was so tired that I was literally dragging my feet), and my hands were in desperate need of lotion. But with a clingy 6-month-old who screamed bloody murder any time I tried to leave the room, there was little time to iron or moisturize.

She had the courage to tell me what other friends had probably noticed but wouldn't dare say. She had a love for me that didn't allow her to stay silent as I walked around looking messy.

I reflected on all of this and softened. My armor cracked and I got real with her (and more importantly, myself).

"I mean, those jeans are the only thing that fit me right now. And… ugh… okay. It's gotten bad. You're right. I'm not taking care of myself like I could be. You're… you're right."

"It's not about being right, I just want…" Andrea try to lift my spirits.

"No," I resisted. "You're right."

I was running on empty, and it had begun to show. I wasn't taking care of myself and everyone around me had noticed, but no one had the courage to tell me. I'd convinced myself that if no one was saying anything, then it must not have been visible, and if it wasn't visible, it wasn't a problem.

But I had completely stopped taking care of myself physically, mentally, and emotionally.

And she cared enough to hold a mirror up to my face and call me out of a messy place.

Sometimes our emotions overtake us, no matter how many yoga classes we've taken and mediation blogs we've read. There's just something about having someone look you in the face and accuse you of being anything other than fabulous. A negative review of our behavior or performance shines a light on our inadequacies, and who wants to look at those? And if a negative comment on your Instagram has the power to get you (a little) worked up, then surely a real-life confrontation about your less-than-best self is going to rattle something inside of you.

Call-outs put us face-to-face with the reality that not everyone appreciates everything about us all the time. They show us that there is room to grow. Call-outs bring to light the shortcomings we'd prefer to keep hidden. And while some of the negative feedback we get is spot on, it still stings.

We now understand that compassion, good timing, receptivity and well-set intentions are important when initiating a difficult conversation. But what do you do when you're on the receiving end? How do you handle someone calling you out on all your Stuff?

TOUGH-LOVE RESPONSE TYPES

After five years of studying and observing female communication patterns, I've identified seven types of tough truth reactions. Depending on your personality and experiences, you likely fall into one of them. We typically gravitate toward one style more than others, and the "life season" we're in at the time of a truth-telling can also affect how we respond.

1. The Great Defender

This reaction style involves defending and justifying everything with great ferocity.

The Great Defender is someone who feels criticism deeply and immediately, and her response is to swat at it— especially if it hits too close to home. It's a swift and natural response, much like the kick in the groin you give to a doctor when she taps your knee with a rubber mallet.

When a doctor taps your knee, that touch messages neurons which message your spinal cord which make your thigh muscles contract. Your leg kicks in response. And the cool thing is that it all happens by reflex, meaning the brain never has to get involved in the process. Your body is on autopilot without it. (Washington.edu)

The Great Defender has this same "knee-jerk response"— she instantly goes to work to protect her bruised ego, and it happens without the brain getting involved in the process. It's just reflex. No matter how the hard truth is packaged, if it smells like criticism, she begins to justify her ways and defend her intentions. Any remarks that "detract" are viewed as an attack on her character, choices, or judgement.

2. The Great Pretender

The Great Pretender initially agrees with hard truths and criticism that she receives. She concedes for the sake of peace and pretends not to be affected by it. In reality, she's bothered by it but doesn't want to cause a ruckus by saying so.

This is typically someone who's uncomfortable with conflict, so she acquiesces in the moment to end the discomfort as much as possible. But her passive agreement isn't genuine. She just gives in to avoid a battle or because she's a people-pleaser, and wants to give you the response that you're looking for.

Another reason she may "pretend" is because she may not have a strong sense of self. This means that she is dependent on others' opinions of her, and those opinions help her to define herself. Even if she receives criticism that's not exactly accurate, she'll consider accepting it because she puts a lot of stock into others' assessments of who she is and what she does.

After leaving the conversation, The Great Pretender will think about what you said and convince herself that she really does agree or quietly stew over the ways she disagrees, which more often than not turns into resentment.

3. The Woman of Splendor

The Woman of Splendor is thrilled about call-outs, believe it or not. She takes joy in being presented with an opportunity for growth, and doesn't take the negative feedback personally. While many others may arrive at this attitude after first showing defensiveness or withdrawal, The Woman of Splendor often expresses her gratitude right away, and goes to work applying the feedback she's received from her friends without being negatively impacted by it.

4. The Energy Spender

This is a girl who has a racing mind and frenetic thoughts. After she's "called-out," she'll exert energy by mulling over what the person said before, during, and certainly after the conversation. She'll likely over-analyze what it meant, how long the person's been feeling that way, what this means for the friendship, and wonder, "Has everybody been thinking that but they're just not telling me?"

The Energy Spender will consider both what was said and what wasn't said. She's looking for subtext and reading it carefully. She will analyze it both while you are speaking and long after you're done. She'll internalize much of what you say, and likely will think past the topic at hand into what you really meant to say. She'll poll her other friends to see if they agree and won't stop until she's dissected the call-out from every angle and has summoned the opinions of all her friends.

5. The Reoffender

The Reoffender will be so embarrassed by her call-out that she begins to double-down. If someone tells her that perhaps she's drinking too much, she'll go out that night and drink even more. If the supervisor she can't stand tells her that her reports are not long enough, her next submission is shorter than ever before. This kind of response happens because she's embarrassed or hurt by the call-out she's received, but instead of assessing what's been said and considering making changes, she'll take on an "I'll show them" attitude.

While most of our responses to criticism demonstrate a lack of emotional maturity, this reaction tends to be the most explicit case. Instead of engaging in the conversation or reflecting on her behavior or attitude, she'll address your call-out by being passive aggressive. "Well, if they think I'm a _____ then I guess I'll be a _____." The Reoffender can't make sense of the message, so she may work to retaliate against the messenger. Ultimately, her response is a manifestation of her own hurt, pride, and embarrassment.

6. Ms. Surrender

When called out, Ms. Surrender won't put up a fight. Perhaps, at most, she'll engage by questioning the "critic's" message, but you'll find that she bends soon afterwards. Most times this is because she has already acknowledged the faults or truths being shared with her, so she's not surprised by or resistant to the tough-love conversation.

The older we get, the more self-aware we become. And while this is not true of everyone, it is generally true of most people. This self-awareness comes from growing more in tune with our faults and weaknesses; recognizing our own patterns, behaviors, and thought processes; and having heard the same feedback from more than one person. So by the time we are called out with a hard truth, Ms. Surrender is likely to have heard it before and is ready to act productively on your feedback.

7. The Willful Suspender

The Willful Suspender will either immediately or gradually suspend her relationship with the one who called her out while she processes the message. She may either immediately begin to put distance between you as she works to avoid a tough love conversation in the first place; or, once invited into a hard conversation, she will try to end it as soon as possible by withdrawing emotionally.

She may also "suspend" the friendship after a tough-love conversation out of discomfort or insecurity, wondering if the one who called her out likes her any less or unsure of her next moves. This separation is often gradual. Sometimes she returns after the temporary "break" and the friendship recovers. Other times, the distance forever shifts the dynamics, and it's too awkward or difficult to return to normal.

HOW TO GET IT RIGHT: ADVICE FROM A BUSINESSWOMAN
I turned to a woman I really admire to share her thoughts on the subject.

Dani Pascarella is Founder and CEO at Invibed, a successful fintech company that provides financial education and wealth coaching to young professionals. She was a stockbroker at the age of 20 while attending the University of Florida, where we met. A Forbes contributor and all-around money maven, she's seriously impressive.

Dani's had to demonstrate resilience and unrelenting ambition to be as successful as she is, so I interviewed her about her views on giving and accepting feedback, as she's undoubtedly experienced her share on her path to success.

Her insight is powerful.

Here's a bit of our conversation:

Q: Do you find that you're having more tough-love conversations with your business partner (Korrie Martinez) since she's also your personal friend?

A: We have tough conversations all the time. It's a part of a growing business where there is a lot to talk about. But it's important to be on the same page. The way I have a conversation with her might differ from how I do it with someone else. It's important to know how everyone receives feedback, because we all do it differently. But honestly, if at the end of the day we are on the same team going for the same thing, it sets the framework. The subject might be tough but we can have the conversation because we genuinely both have the same goal. When you realign to being on the same team, then it makes it easier to give and accept difficult feedback.

Q: You mention having a framework that guides your conversation.

What do you mean by that and how does it help you?

A: *Having a framework for giving feedback is something I always do. People always like to say things before thinking it through, but [you have to first consider] "What's the objective? What's the outcome I'm hoping to get?" Then usually it's the wording that's going to help get the person that thing. Usually what I take the time to come up with is different than what I'd say if I went off the cuff. It should never come from an emotional state. It seldom ends well.*

Q: In your position, you may have to give negative feedback to those you work with. But how do you handle tough criticism yourself?

A. Being an example is an important thing. With women there is an expectation that you have to be perfect. Men are taught that you can make mistakes but with women have this "I need to be perfect," and call-outs pierce that. So its important to create a culture where its okay to fail.

I try to be very conscious about what I'm good at and what I'm not. I try not to be perfect. When I'm getting bad feedback.

I think frameworks are the key to life. I grew up as a perfectionist, so I know that if I get feedback, I have to be alone to process it because I know my reaction will be better once I process it. I was in an accelerator program when I got started, and we went through 3-5 of those [feedback evaluations] every day for 6 weeks. I had to come up with a framework or I wouldn't last.

I write down my take-ways. It's always jarring, it's never fun, but remember they are trying to help you and make you better. Then take time to process. A skill I've spent time working on is "the bounce back period" – at least, that's what I call it. I've literally sat down and tried to decrease the bounce back period. I'll think "Man I'm really rattled by this", then go take a walk and go to gym. And then I actually test what would make me feel better. I used to stew on it, but now its 2-10 minutes because it's like a muscle.

Q: It sounds like you take a really systematic approach to something that, for most people, is a matter of emotion. Do you think this technical approach works beyond the professional realm?

A. I cant think of one time I put a process in place and thought "I regret doing this". Our minds are really easy to shape and if you put in the time and effort you can teach yourself to think how you want.

Think about trading on Wall Street. We are very emotional; if you're emotional then you're not going to make the best decision. But if you have a process, you stick to no matter what. Traders do this on Wall Street. Stick to the process. They don't respond to the chaos by saying, "I'm feeling anxious so I'll do this on stock."

But it's not just in business. Even when it comes to a friend choosing to be with a guy I'm not necessarily fond of—I've used the exact same approach in giving feedback: We're on the same team and I want you to be successful in finding the right partner. Human psychology is human psychology. I don't care where you are.

HOW TO GET IT RIGHT: ADVICE FROM A COMMUNICATION COACH

Another perspective on taking a tough love truth-telling?

I reached out to Telana Simpson, a highly respected life coach living and working in South Africa. She specifically helps people in the areas of communicating and relating, improving their skills and feelings surrounding conflict, confrontation, and developing relationships.

I knew right away she'd be the perfect person to ask about how women can better manage their responses to a tough love truth-telling from a girlfriend:

Q: How do we re-frame our minds to see feedback from friends as helpful instead of offensive?

A: It's nice to have someone close to you give feedback in a loving, tender way so that you can actually learn and grow. They put up with you because they're your friend. That's the power of coaching. Your friends won't always do that because they're your friends. They're trying to make you feel better... But with real true friends... it depends on the level of friendship you want with that person. Maybe you're doing them a favor by giving them some feedback.

Q: So what do you say to the person getting "called out"?

A: Well hopefully that person's read your book. Ha!

If it's delivered in a constructive way, it's much easier for it to land. But if it's not given in a constructive way, there's a whole lot of skills they can develop where its easier to take it— even if the person [giving it is] not skilled.

Even then, just remember that it's their *perspective— it's* their *view.*

Q: And how are we to respond, what are we to say, when we've gotten negative feedback that takes us by surprise?

A: Whatever it is say, "Can I have a bit of time to process this?"

With tough conversations, we think we have to solve it all straight away. Sometimes we need time to process what the emotions are— for them to go through our system, so that we can understand what the person is actually trying to say. Maybe even saying, 'I'm upset by what you said, I just need time to process this. Can I get back to you?" If you feel like you can't process, give yourself a break. Try to ask more questions. It's just their perspective.

But if it's a friend, they know you really well because you've spent so much time together. Just ask more about it: "What leads you to have this opinion about me?" or "I've never thought of it like that..." And not with the purpose to agree or disagree with them, but to UNDERSTAND where it's coming from— what it actually means.

Q: How do we find the good in what our friend is saying when on the surface, it's initially hurtful?

A: You might find a good nugget in what they say, and then you can throw out the rest because you realize that it's their stuff and their triggers. If you value the friendship, then ask for the time and space to process to ask the questions for clarity, and even ask for that person's help — if they're your friend.

Q: You keep going back to one thing: asking questions. So often we respond to criticism with defensiveness or anxiety because we don't know what to say. But you encourage women to re-think the way they view feedback altogether in order to really make the most of it. And that comes by asking. Is that right?

A. That goes for the person giving and getting [tough love truth-tellings]. Try to understand before you judge what that person's saying. Lose the assumptions and try to understand. Ask questions for clarity. And our natural reaction is to defend ourselves. The questioning is not assuming you know everything. You should be questioning the other person— you actually learn a lot more and you have more understanding.

Sure, it's helpful when someone gives you a gentle call-out and delivers negative feedback in a constructive way. But true emotional maturity is being able to take feedback even when it's given poorly, even when a person's intentions are to [hurt]. The key is not letting their lack of tenderness or emotional intelligence get in the way of you extracting the parts that could actually help you improve.

QUICK TIPS FOR TAKING TOUGH FEEDBACK

1. **You don't have to respond right away.** Give yourself a break. This is a key point that Telana made during our interview, and I have found that putting it into practice is actually very liberating.

2. Try to look at **feedback as data**. It's very hard when emotions are involved, yes. But if we train ourselves to accept it as more information to include as we work toward constant self-improvement, it could be helpful.

3. **Measure the feedback** you're getting against patterns. Are other people saying the same thing to you? Have you heard this message more than once? If so, it may be valid.

4. Remember that **listening to your friend is not the same as agreeing** with her. Find a way to hear what she's saying without being combative. You have the right to disagree with her opinion afterwards—and to continue to like her anyway.

5. **Pay attention.** Examine the person's intentions. Does this friend typically

have your best interest at heart? Does she love to see you win? If so, then weigh her "call-out" against her spirit of encouragement and try to see the negative feedback as an extension of her love for you, not contradictory to it.

In a strong friendship, there is space for each person to learn, grow, and take the time they need. This is central to the *Challenging* sector of the Tough-Love Friendship Model. When called out by a friend, it is okay to tell them the conversation is too difficult for you if you find that you're unable to manage it in real-time. It's okay to ask if you can pick it up later or to request the time you need to process what they're saying to you.

If a friend is pressuring you to listen to what she has to say and then to pivot immediately, she is not exercising the patience and grace that's required among friends. Since not everyone has the maturity or emotional intelligence to realize this is what they may be doing, you must have the courage to help make her aware by asking for what you need. If you need more time, tell her. Is the conversation too difficult? Say so. Are you not in the right head space to receive the message she's sharing with you? Let her know.

True and loving friendship will make room.

When You're Wary of Her Choices

I've had a series of men I'd like to forget, and every time I got involved with one of them, my friends naturally disapproved.

My high school boyfriend was an attractive football player and had a smile that made my knees buckle. All I knew at the time was that when he looked at me I felt like the coolest, most beautiful girl in the world.

When he broke his gaze and looked elsewhere, I immediately questioned if my beauty had somehow faded along with his interest. Despite him treating me like a number, I stuck around because being "chosen" made me feel special.

Then came my college boyfriend, a "creative." He wrote music and lyrics that were addictively clever. Despite his dishonesty and affinity for weed, I stuck around because being with him awakened a new rebellion inside of me.

The last man I dated before I met my husband was handsome and athletic. The five-year age difference made me see him as a "wise, older guy" and my 23-year-old self just couldn't shake him. Despite his belittling and controlling behavior, I stuck around because I was dysfunctionally attracted to his "alpha" male energy.

There were several other men between the athlete, the musician, and the older man. With each of these relationships, I explored a new version of myself, despite being overlooked, used, or mislead.

My friends watched it all from the outside, forming their judgments and opinions about my chosen man: whether he was worth my time, whether he was likable, whether I was happy.

During each relationship, my friends saw clearly what I refused to admit:

My boyfriend was awful.

But each time, they were unsure of the authority they had as my friends and rarely voiced concerns about the ways I was being undervalued and mistreated. The few who dared to express their disapproval were met with resistance and defensiveness because they either approached me with a unapologetic brashness or came to me lovingly— but I was so insecure I couldn't really listen to the rational truth they were dropping on me.

My situation was not unique. When I was teaching 18-year-old's, girls often told me (explicitly or implicitly) about their friends' newest beau and all the ways he wasn't good enough. In my social circles and as a women's coach, I listen as women express their frustration with their friends.

Try your best to examine some of the reasons she may have attached to him:

He makes her feel loved, something she has not experienced recently.

He is introducing her to new things (whether they are dangerous or productive, it doesn't matter. Sometimes it's just the thrill of something new). The relationship makes her feel important. Or maybe he really is just wonderful.

Think twice about sharing your concern for you friend's latest love interest. If you decide it really is worth addressing, there are a few things you've got to do before you have the tough love conversation she may need:

1. Get to know him. Is it possible he actually is a good guy, but you don't know that because you just haven't spent enough time getting familiar with him? You may find that you're mistaken about his motives and personality, simply because you you don't know him well enough. Don't be afraid to suggest the three of you hang out so that you have a chance to see up-close what he's like.

2. Check your preferences. It's possible that he is a good guy and has the best intentions for your girl, but you just don't like his personality. And if this is

the case, I have to break it to you: It doesn't matter. If your friend is being well cared for and she enjoys the relationship, then the jokes you find obnoxious or the shyness that makes you skeptical are just a part of the package. Be sure to examine the difference between your personal preferences and your friend's best interest. And when she marries the guy, just stand at the altar beside her, smile, and be happy that your friend has found someone she loves.

3. And when at odds with your friend's new guy, evaluate your motivation. Are you simply jealous of the time you're losing with her because of his arrival, or are you genuinely concerned about his threat to her well being? If you find that it's a matter of feeling boxed out, it may not be in your head.

Remember the "Rule of 150" by Robin Dunbar that I outlined in the intimacy chapter? It suggests that we can only maintain 150 people in our network at a time, with only 5 of those being our close "core" people. Well, Robin Dunbar also studied the impact of romantic relationships on friendship and found that is having a boyfriend, it takes the place of TWO "inner core" spots— quite literally, the blossoming romance could cost us friends.

I'd like to think that this is a reason we feel, on some biological level, initially threatened when our friend introduces a new guy into her life. There are only so many hours in a day, and now she's got to find a way to divide them between more people. Something's got to give.

I share this to let you know that it's not in your head—if there is any part of you that's not exactly thrilled by her new boyfriend, it's totally normal and expected. But if you're calling her out from a place of personal insecurity, you're gonna have to check yourself.

Just sayin'.

WHEN HER BOYFRIEND'S NOT THE THING YOU DISAPPROVE OF

I focus so much on men in a chapter about our friends' choices, because the survey I conducted this revealed this to be the number one decision where women find it difficult to support their friends.

But we know this goes beyond disliking our friends' new guy.

Here are some things to keep in mind, regardless of the specific disagreement at hand:

Close friendship gives us front row seats to the good and bad in someone's life, and with such access and insight it's easy to form strong opinions about what it is we (think we) see. Whether it's her choice of men, her overindulgence with alcohol, the way she parents... we find ourselves disapproving some of her choices— and then wondering whether or not we should say anything.

Determining whether or not to confront our friend with a concern about her decisions is so delicate because the last thing we want to do is pass judgment. This clearly falls within the *Challenging* sector of tough-love friendship because it requires that we address hard truths with a friend. When it's time to hold her accountable, we sometimes think twice about what to do, if anything at all. And for alpha females, who eagerly share their opinion of a friend's choices, it's often done in a way that is less of an invitation to dialogue and more of a judgement or accusation.

This type of situation, while predominately of the *Challenging* sector, is somewhat connected to each of the Tough-Love Friendship Model sectors:

a. Having heard her secret fears, insecurities, and emotions, we work to help her tend to them and take action that will keep those spaces safe by calling out choices she makes that may threaten the very well being we care so much about (*Sharing* sector).

b. If she has expressed a boundary, the "call-out" we give her is our attempt to help her maintain them. We uphold our own boundaries by letting her know we don't want to sit by and watch her put herself in physical or emotional danger— that it's something we won't do (*Preserving* sector).

c. As you champion your friend, reminding her of her worth, it makes sense that we'd confront her concerning decisions if we believe they'd detract from her awesomeness (*Affirming* sector).

HOW TO SHOW SUPPORT WHEN YOU DISAGREE

Disagreeing with the choices our friends make is inevitable. The key is to find a way to support her anyway, because this girl needs you to have her back.

Here are three ways to show up for your friend even when you disagree with her.

1. Identify the parts you do support. Many times an argument is so nuanced that there are bound to be aspects of her position that you can agree with. Try your best to home in on those parts and do your best to amplify them. That's what true support looks like.

Ex 1: She's going on a date with a total downgrade. Good for her for getting out there—get manis together the day before and suggest a good date spot.

Ex 2: She's chasing after a job or dream that you think is a bad fit. Good for her for being ambitious—buy her a book like *Money Management for Millennials* by Merrie Allmon Allen to get her started.

Ex 3: She wants to have a medical procedure, but you just can't stand behind it. Be there for her physically and emotionally afterwards to help her recover, if necessary.

Ex 4: She said "Yes" to the wrong guy. Buy her cutesy "Engaged" shirts and mugs and other bridal trinkets—she's excited and wants you to be excited with her.

Ex 5: Her new friends are not your cup of tea. Save an occasional Friday night to join them out on the town. If that's too much to handle, then occasionally ask her how they're doing (and try your best to mean it).

Ex 6: You find her parenting style to be a little ridiculous. Hey, "momming" is hard. As long as her kids are not being emotionally or physically abused, suck it up and schedule mommy time for you two to get away from your little rugrats for a few hours.

WHEN YOU'RE WARY OF HER CHOICES

The key is to emphasize your concern with the issue at hand and avoid the temptation to judge her character or decision-making, because that is the single fastest way to get shut down.

2. Find the right time and place, then talk about it.

You cannot avoid this issue or beat around the bush—true friends are able to keep it real with each other (with a bit of grace, of course). If it is the first conversation you're having with your friend about said issue and she seems completely excited about whatever it is she is sharing with you, vocalizing your concern (at that time) in low doses may be best— you don't want to kill the girl's vibe. It's also possible that you haven't had the time to process the information and thoughtfully choose the best words.

So before you say anything, find the right time. Maybe you can wait until you've just had a belly laugh over cocktails and ease into things. Or hey, sometimes it's best to wait a few days and call her up.

Bring it up with a lead-in like:

"I've been thinking about this _____ thing you shared with me the other day and I'm kind of worried because _____. I love you and the last thing I want is for this to cause any _____ between us, but because I want the best for you, I just have to stress that _____. I'll have your back either way."

The key is to emphasize your concern with the **issue** at hand while avoiding the temptation to make judgments on her **decision-making**, because that is the single fastest way to get shut down.

If you can't express your concerns to your friend, I'm going to just say that you may want to reassess that your relationship altogether. Is there a reason you feel so uneasy about sharing your truth? Is it because she's combative or are you especially sensitive to the fears of abandonment and confrontation? Have you invested enough in the friendship to make a "withdrawal" when you challenge her choices? But if verbalizing your disagreement is something you are ready to do, there is right way to do things to keep your friendship still intact.

3. Pray about it.

Yep, seriously. Chances are, despite your very sound and logical argument, you may be wrong yourself, my dear. It's our suggestion that you ask for guidance (to know what to say), compassion (to see things from her side), and humility (so you can listen to her with your heart instead of quick and dismissive judgement).

We have to be slow to speak, and practice really listening. We don't always have the right answers. Seeking direction is the best thing you can do instead of leaning into your own understanding and perspective. The guidance you receive may lead you to a place you weren't expecting.

You can also ask for her to be granted wisdom and courage, along with physical and emotional protection.

Now, it goes without saying that if the decision your friend is making concerns her physical or emotional well-being, there is no tip-toeing around it—you need to explicitly state your disapproval and emphasize your concern for her safety. Get the interventions you need to make sure your girl is okay.

KEEPING PERSPECTIVE

When your friend is making decisions that don't necessarily align with your choices, remember: we are all different, and regardless of her choices, she needs you by her side. Do your best to find a way to see past the moves she's making and, instead, have her back along the way. This falls into the *Challenge* sector of tough-love friendship because after you courageously invite her into a conversation about her choices, you allow her to exercise her independence and maintain an emotional connection in the midst of divergence— a true sign of a relationship with love and acceptance.

If you're quick to voice your opinion and express your disapproval, yield to the power of dialogue and make an effort to ask more questions— talk less. If you've weighed the situation thoughtfully, engaged her, and still feel lead to approach the issue by tending to the *Challenging* sector of tough-love friendship, remember to do show with patience and love.

WHY YOU HAVE TO SHOW UP

The friend who doesn't express concern when she sees glaring issues is complicit. She's allowing the problem to continue through passive avoidance. Non-negotiable issues you should address are verbal, physical, and emotional abuse and manipulation— and if the relationship in any way makes her feel badly about herself, it is your responsibility to invite her into a conversation about it.

And being a tough love friend is not just meant to benefit the friend hearing the hard truth; it's also designed to benefit you. In order to feel liberated in your friendship and free in your personal truth, you have to share it. It may feel awkward and it could temporarily rattle the comfortable ecosystem you and your friend have created, but it's so worth it. In fact, "difficult, but worth it" typically describes most of the things in life worth having.

If you do choose to enter into a hard truth conversation with your friend, remember to apply the S.E.T the M.I.C framework before you invite her into dialogue about the situation:

Does the problem have a solution? Is the environment appropriate? Have you set the right tone? Have you examined your motivation and intentions? Have you invested in her before the conversation and are you ready to stay invested with her afterwards? Does she have the capacity to receive your message?

Remember, it's not possible to agree with all of your friend's choices. (If you do happen to agree with everything, I'd encourage you to explore the degree to which you are simply acquiescing and how much of your authentic self you've brought to that friendship. This would mean staying true to the *Sharing* and *Challenging* sectors of tough-love friendship.)

To experience true intimacy in your friendship, there has to be room for you each to make choices that the other may disagree with. The trick is to confront each other where appropriate, and then to love each other along the way.

When Insecurities Get in the Way

I had a coaching session with a woman whose complaint was that her friend was an overachieving perfectionist who "just wants to impress people." The woman I was speaking with— we'll call her Jamie— was visibly aggravated by her friend's obsessive tendencies.

My first order of business was to help Jamie see that her issue wasn't with her friend's annoying habit of perfection— it was with her own insecurities of not feeling like enough in comparison.

As friends, we come to know each other so well that we feel like we can practically diagnose their issues, obnoxious habits, family history, and personal preferences. But sometimes we have to put aside the familiarity (that we often overestimate)- and approach our friend with the curiosity of someone meeting her for the first time. It's not until we can humble ourselves to do this that we better understand what motivates her.

Jaime shouldn't have been caught up in her girlfriend's incessant perfectionism, but it was a delicate issue for one reason: Jaime's personal insecurities of not feeling good enough.

When I was teaching my high school seniors, we read William Shakespeare's tragic play *Othello*. One of the key themes in the play is jealousy, and there's a line that villain Iago says that gives me goosebumps every time I read it: Referring to an upstanding character named Cassio, Iago says, "He hath a daily beauty in his life which makes me ugly." And while women balk at the "u" word, Iago is speaking to the feeling of inferiority— someone whose mere existence makes us feel small by comparison.

The tragedy in Jaime's misjudgment of her friend's issue is that both women were being motivated by their secret insecurities: Her friend was driven to accomplish tasks because her self-worth was based on praise. Jaime was increasingly jealous (although she would never admit to it— we rarely do) because her friend's accomplishments awakened her private feelings of inadequacy.

SECRET FEARS AND COMMUNICATION

Despite the bond we may feel with other women, it's often no match for the secret fear we carry. And when our respective insecurities are activated by misunderstandings, disagreements, or lack of communication, it can affect the way tough love friendship is supposed to work.

Let me be clear: We all have insecurities. I don't care what anyone says. Due to our experiences, varying attachment styles, and self-perceived shortcomings, we are all doing what we can to navigate life with our respective insecurities. We may manage them differently, but we're all dealing with seasons of confidence and uncertainty. We're all dealing with our own Stuff.

Remember, tough-love friendship speaks honestly and holds each girl accountable (the Challenging sector of the Tough-Love Friendship Model). But that becomes distorted when we're offering and receiving "tough-love" through a hazy lens of self-conscious sensitivities. The message won't be given or received authentically.

There was a time when I heard "insecure" and immediately pictured a meek girl with furrowed eyebrows and a mousy voice walking around saying, "Do you like me? Do you like me?" The illustration I held of an insecure woman was the more obvious image, envisioning a woman who was unsure of herself, her relationship, or her surroundings. But as the years went on and I navigated social circles in college, then observed thousands of students over my years as an educator, and later still, interacting with my clients at STRIDE Media Group, I now understand how insecurity is a shape-shifter. It can operate as a confident businesswoman or masquerade as a laser-focused straight-A student. Insecurity is a pretender and it drives so much of what we do (and don't do).

This includes our friendships.

Why is a chapter about insecurities relevant in a book about tough-love friendships? Because for some, every aspect of how we operate is rooted in insecurity, both within ourselves and the friend we want to draw near to. Because we are all girls out here trying to make it, and we have to keep that in mind when we enter into new friendships.

Let's look at how it affects each sector of the Tough-Love Friendship Model:

Sharing: If you feel insecure about being lovable enough and fear rejection, it will prevent you from having the courage to be vulnerable.

Preserving: Not feeling comfortable in your own skin or lacking a strong sense of self will prevent you from firmly establishing and communicating your boundaries.

Affirming: Those who lack confidence in themselves often find it difficult to affirm others, feeling it somehow detracts from their own value.

Challenging: Fearing abandonment and rejection will drive an urge to avoid conflict in a relationship, preventing women from confidently holding friends accountable.

The key is to do the work to identify your personal insecurities and to examine how they may be sabotaging your friendships.

When you're confronting your friend about a comment, attitude, or behavior that makes you uncomfortable, it can be unfair if you haven't taken the time to objectively assess whether or not your issue is with her attitude or if your concern stems from personal insecurities. If a friend calls you out on something that hits too close to home regarding something you're sensitive about, you'll likely respond defensively.

A TALE OF TWO WOMEN

So let's look at an example of how this can play out.

Jamie found herself bothered by Rachel's perfectionism.

Rachel was up at 4:00AM each day so that she had time to go to the gym, get her kids dressed in the cutest, most Insta-worthy outfits, and get herself dressed well for work. She often volunteered to take on additional projects in the office, and she spent social time leading book clubs and hosting small gatherings.

Jamie told me that she was initially drawn to Rachel because she was warm and inviting, but she'd gradually grown tired of the way Rachel took on too much and strove to live a life without error.

"I see how she's killin' herself to please ad 'wow' us. It's always packaged like she's taking one for the team, like she's doing us a favor. But she's not a martyr, she's a masochist. And wants to make it look like it's such a breeze but I see how she's buried under the weight of it all. She's probably working so hard to try to compete with us or something…"

Jamie tried to articulate exactly what is was about Rachel's "striving" that bothered her, and she interpreted Rachel's efforts with competition instead of seeing it for what it was: Rachel's need for validation.

Rachel was annoyed because she perceived Jamie's increasing push-back as jealousy.

I empathized with both women.

Rachel had fallen victim to a culture that praises exhaustion and preaches that doing more is the mark of ambition and success. Believing the lie, Rachel's on the brink of burnout, yet has found her identity in "doing all the things." It makes her feel useful When she hosts parties, she feels loved and important. When she coordinates her children's outfits, she feels seen.

As Rachel struggles for validation, Jaime struggles with feelings of invisibility and inadequacy. The juxtaposition of these two women only emphasizes their respective insecurities. But each is so consumed with her own perception of the other's motivation, that they're missing an opportunity to bond over insecurities that essentially boil down to the same issue: a desire to be seen. Ironically, it's in each other that this desire can actually be met, as they affirm and encourage one other.

CHECK YOUR INSECURITIES SO YOU CAN SHOW UP

If only Jamie took the time to really see her friend, to invite her to a conversation about her overworking. If only she empathized with Rachel's secret desire to be seen instead of being irritated and intimidated by behavior that was only a symptom of a greater problem.

If we put our own insecurities aside and approach our friends humbly, we may be able to show up for them in a better way, honoring our friendship in the process.

Jamie missed an opportunity to compassionately tell Rachel that overworking is often read as hard work and that she was worried about her— especially when burnout was recently recognized as an actual medical diagnosis (World Health Organization 2019).

If Jamie allowed herself to see Rachel with less accusation or more curiosity, she'd recognize her obsessive busyness (and accompanying exhaustion) for what it was, extending a more compassionate view. Instead of a tough-love conversation that accuses (*I don't know why you keep trying to go over the top to impress everyone...*) it could have been one that questions, encourages, and uplifts (*I'm worried you're overextending yourself. How can I support you?*)

Recognizing and checking her own insecurities would directly impact the way Jamie was able to show up for Rachel. It would change the conversation, and ultimately deepen their overall friendship.

How many opportunities have we missed to draw closer to other women because our insecurities were affecting our abilities to tend to each critical sector of the Tough-Love Friendship Model? How many times have we unknowingly been victims of the invisible force driving us away from being vulnerable (*Sharing* sector) and erecting boundaries (*Preserving* sector)? Have we missed out on close connections because our insecurities didn't allow us to pour into other women the way they needed (*Affirming* sector), or to keep them accountable in a way that helped them to grow (*Challenging* sector)?

WHEN INSECURITIES GET IN THE WAY

Tough-love calls for you to check your own insecurities so as not to have your friendships be anything less than wonderful, liberating relationships.

Calling it Out: Gossip and Complaining

It feels a little silly to admit, but I was just so freaking eager.

It was the summer between my sophomore and junior year of college and I was sitting on the bed with one of the most beautiful girls I'd ever laid my eyes on. I knew her because she was friends with my boyfriend, but I'd never expected to be spending one-on-one time with her.

Her name was Bianca, and she'd come to college with six close girlfriends. These chicks did everything together— and their constant posts on Facebook (IG wasn't that big at the time) were evidence of their amazingness. You'd occasionally spot photos of them with an "outsider" at a party, but typically they were in perfectly coordinated form— just the six of them— leaving us all wondering what our own regular, down-home friend groups were missing. Several girls had attempted to break into their tight circle, but they were "no new friends" before Drake even dropped his first mixtape.

I'd also always admired Bianca's beauty and her large, happy friend group from the outside. I think I knew they probably had their own issues like everyone else, but still, a part of me bought the hype: They were an exclusive group of melanated bombshells and were #SquadGoals before hashtags were even a thing.

So the magnitude of the moment wasn't lost on me when she texted and asked if I'd come hang out one-on-one at her apartment. I knew it was a pity invite because none of her other friends were enrolled for summer classes— they were all back in their hometown of Boston.

Although I was having a good time taking in her glamorous presence, trendy closet and lavish attention, I became awkward when she shifted from girly pleasantries to something else: secrets about her friends. The girls in the "Sexy Six."

"… I mean, she's supposed to be Ms. Perfect but she had an abortion three months ago. I'm not sharing that with a lot of people obviously, because it's private, but it's hard because she puts on this act of being better than others when she has secrets like the rest of us, you know?"

I was speechless. Embarrassed for her friend, I stayed silent, unwilling to participate but not wanting the attention to end.

"And Laura is my closest friend in the group, but lately she's been kinda gravitating to Lex, which is cool, but I think it's just because they're both in relationships now and feel bonded over that— whatever. I mean, I think Laura's boyfriend isn't exactly faithful, so their relationships aren't on the same level, but I get how these new relationships are bringing the girls together. That's fine. I seriously don't care, I'm happy for them. It just changes things, you know?"

Just listening made me feel guilty. These were things I wasn't supposed to know. And although I felt somehow complicit, I also felt privileged to have access to secrets about the most enviable group of girls on campus.

As enamored I was by the moment we were sharing, I wondered if the girls in her circle operated like this on the regular. I wondered if those of us who admired them had been fooled this whole time, and the girls in the "Sexy Six" were nothing more than a collective mirage, and in reality were a co-dependent band of girls who gossiped about each other once the camera flashes faded away.

When the exchange was over, I headed back to my lonely dorm room (summer classes are lonely, do you hear me?) and I began thinking about why we gossip with our friends… and about our friends.

This is important now as I explore tough-love friendships because:

1. Tough-love friendships call out behavior that can be detrimental to the individual woman involved in the friendship

2. Tough-love friendship refuses to participate in exchanges that could negatively impact her or others, despite how hard it can be to not give in

Gossip tends to require both of these, so let's explore it.

WHY GOSSIP IS SO SEDUCTIVE

As disenchanted as I was over the dulling luster I'd held when I viewed the "Sexy Six," I knew that gossip wasn't unique to their group.

Gossip is powerful because when we share intel about a friend, stranger or co-worker, it feels like a secret. And there is something powerful about a shared secret. It connects us and we're brought together through this little piece of knowledge we're not supposed to have. It's seductive.

But what do you do when you have a friend who loves to gossip and you're dying to call her out on it? How do you show tough love to a friend who's always dishing about others? How do you stay out of it? And is it even your job to call her out, or do you just chalk it up to her personality and accept it (even though you squirm and look at her sideways each time she opens her mouth to badmouth someone)? And the biggest question of all: How do you stop it when you enjoy participating in it with her?

Let me be clear: Gossip is not just something that mean-spirited girls engage in. If you get the image of a feisty and conniving woman when you hear the word "gossip," allow me to challenge that picture. The truth is that even the most compassionate, well-meaning woman will find herself chatting about other people.

Why?

The cornerstone of human connection is conversation. And one of the most common topics of conversation is other people. This doesn't necessarily mean it's malicious, but it's only natural, as our lives are made up with our exchanges with, thoughts about, and feelings concerning other human beings.

From a sociological aspect, gossip is not a crazy concept. Most of our conversation is people-centric anyway. A slow slip into exchanging unflattering information filled with speculation is not a far leap from innocent chatter about the people we know.

The problem comes when there is deception and disloyalty involved. If your girlfriend is always "speculating" about others, it's makes you wonder if you can trust her with the secret parts of your life, too. If you and a friend quietly chat about another friend's behavior but when in front of said friend you present as if you support her behavior, it creates a distorted reality.

The difference between "people talk" and "gossip" is that gossip often includes reports about people that haven't been confirmed as true. It's when you share information that is largely speculation, and could therefore be detrimental to the person's reputation (or actual livelihood, depending on the content).

One is a basic sociological behavior. The other? A problem.

How do we handle this with tough-love?

WHY YOU HAVE TO CALL IT OUT

<u>You have to call it out for your friend's sake.</u> It's an unspoken belief that the person who's constantly talking about other people can't be trusted. While her audience may listen with hungry curiosity, they're also making mental notes that they have to be careful around her, lest they give her some of their own business to share. As your friend, you shouldn't want her to be in a position where others are leery of her. And as such an unattractive quality, the gossip is something positioning her as a threat to others because, surely, others will keep her at arms' length.

She may also need you to make her aware of the habit because she doesn't even realize she's doing it. Remember, before approaching any tough-love conversation, you should consider giving the benefit of the doubt.

You may want to burst with, "Damn, Jaclyn, all you do is run your mouth about other people!" But is it possible that she's completely oblivious? Gossiping is so ingrained in our speech that we don't realize it's a problem. And it's hard to recognize it as a problem when people respond to it. And if she isn't aware of how bad it's gotten, who's going to tell her? The only ones qualified is the people who care about her most.

<u>You have to call it out for your sake.</u> If the gossiping really bothers you, but you refuse to say anything, you are going to express your concern one way or another. So often we work to convince ourselves that if we don't say

anything that things will work themselves out. And sometimes, that happens. But if an issue really makes you uncomfortable, it's going to show one way or another.

You will either find yourself creating physical distance, going silent when she gossips—leaving her to wonder what she did wrong; or having increasing frustration as your internal conflict grows every time she indulges. This is why it may be best that you tell her how you feel, inviting her into a conversation about the habit.

<u>You have to call it out for the sake of your friendship.</u> If your friend's tendency to gossip is something that has you looking at her with growing suspicion (*Does she talk about me too?*), it's going to inevitably strain your relationship. Instead of leaving her to wonder why there's an occasional emotional distance between you two, it may be best to chat about it outright.

Your friendship also suffers because we are all leery of the friend who is known for speaking about other people. It makes us wonder if she's doing the same to us. (Spoiler alert: She is.) If you are keeping an emotional guard up because you can't trust that she'll keep your business private and your secrets confidential, then you'll obviously be less likely to share. You'll find yourself measuring what you say with caution, because you have no confidence in her ability to keep your information just between the two of you. Whenever anyone withholds from another, it impedes on their level of intimacy, and you'll never be as close to your girl as you could be if you're always working to protect yourself from her.

Other ways you can show tough love:
- Refuse to indulge her when she works to draw you into a conversation about someone else.
- Respond with something like, "No, I hadn't heard about her Tanya's money issues, but girl, I know if people were talking about my money issues I'd be mortified."
- Give her space. If you're in a group setting, turn to another friend and engage her in conversation instead. This way, the gossip-attempt falls flat.
- Blame yourself. "You know what, I'm trying to be better about gossiping

so, girl, I just can't."

Now, don't get me wrong, I have participated in this very fully. I mean, there was a point when this was one of my FAVORITE things to do with my friends. But the more I realized how hurtful it became (not only to those of us gossiping, but to those we were talking about) I began to feel more and more convicted about it.

WHEN THINGS GET NEGATIVE

Another common friendship issue that we struggle to confront: Complaining and negativity. And I feel a little twinge of conviction when I bring this up because it makes me recall my own experience... but here it is:

It was funny at first.

Karen and I made dark, sarcastic comments about our job—the monotony of each task, the idiocy of our co-workers. Initially it was just some mutual venting, and we justified it by fixating on the fact that our job really was terrible and our supervisors truly were awful people. But the cynical commentary gradually leaked outside of the workplace, and I found myself complaining about—well, everything.

And I'm still astounded by how gradually it happened. It's kind of like when you go swimming in the ocean and, letting the waves move you with each push, you look up suddenly and realize you've drifted far beyond the beach towel and umbrella that you laid out as place markers.

The negativity that surrounded me are the waves, in this scenario.

Eventually, a friend pointed out that I didn't seem happy because I'd been "complaining" a lot, and she hesitated to use the word. Perhaps it's because it almost feels like he ultimate insult. To hear people tell you that you're a complainer? Ouch. It's embarrassing, and it certainly bruises your pride. Who wants to be a Debbie Downer?

While I experienced this bitterness in a temporary season of joylessness, there are those who have made complaining a way of life.

These people are everywhere. And they're not just the women we don't like—some of them are our very best friends.

It turns out I wasn't alone.

WHEN THE PESSIMISM CREEPS IN

The 2019 survey I conducted among Millennial women revealed that 53% of women have experienced friendship with a woman who was always complaining.

But how do you tell a friend that she's too negative? How do you call out a defeatist attitude (consistently expecting failure and demise) without striking a nerve or getting hit with defensiveness? And can we even blame her for her negativity? Is her pessimistic attitude even her fault?

Here is why "negativity call-outs" are difficult: there is a thin, blurry line between occasional cathartic venting and constant "Scrooge-like" grumbling. It's hard to encourage someone to eliminate the habit when there is so much about complaining that actually draws us together.

Before I began STRIDE Media Group, I spent seven years as a high school teacher. I made many of my work friends by chatting about our unsupportive administration, disrespectful students and challenging parents. We became a refuge for each other. I found understanding in my co-workers. They were the only ones who knew what it was like to be passionate about your career but resentful of the conditions of your job. We were also tragically overworked and underpaid.

Sharing our grievances drew us closer, with some of us beginning to spend time together beyond the confines of tiny classrooms. We went to happy hours together, and soon we were attending each other's birthday parties, and the talk often turned negative every time. Even with some of my closest teacher friends, I found myself eventually needing a time out, because the complaining was beginning to affect my entire day. (Let me just say, until teachers get the kind of professional and emotional support they need, they have a lot to complain about. I just hadn't figured out my boundaries for productive venting and an ongoing pessimistic attitude.)

Whether bound to our friends from work, college, or as neighbors, there is something pleasant about complaining together. But how do we handle it when the negativity goes too far and we find ourselves dreading being around the other person? What do we do when the negativity begins to affect the way we feel about the overall friendship?

FEELING STRESSED? STOP COMPLAINING.

Roberty Sapolsky, a neurology professor at Stanford, conducted a study in 2016 and found that complaining releases cortisol, the hormone that causes stress. While occasional venting can make us feel relieved, constant complaining can actually make you feel worse. But it doesn't only affect the person complaining—it affects the person listening.

The study also found that complaining literally erodes your brain over time, specifically the part that is responsible for your ability to problem-solve. This is important because it shows that after complaining long enough, you've literally made it more difficult to figure out a way out of the very situations you're complaining about!

By definition it seems so harmless: *complain (v.) to express dissatisfaction.* But it turns out that between the neurological, physical, and emotional fallout of (constant) complaining is detrimental not only to the one doing it, but to those they're in relationships with.

TIPS TO STOP COMPLAINTS IN THEIR TRACKS

Let's be clear: Vulnerably opening up about fears and frustrations is healthy and normal. We sometimes have to talk it through to feel better and figure out a way to approach our problems. But an ongoing attitude of "Everything sucks" is an issue.

I personally know why it's important to begin redirecting friends who are negative: It causes undue stress and tension if you don't. I found that my friendship was suffering because I was letting it go unchecked. Before I had the courage (and the strategies) to redirect my friend

* I didn't pick up the phone when my "downer" friend called.
* I began thinking of reasons (read: lies) of what I was suddenly unable to meet up for coffee.
* Conversations with her became full of landmines.

* I didn't feel good after we hung out. I felt exhausted.

Here are a few tips to try when you're friends with a woman whose negative is getting you down:

1. Create a new boundary, but present it as doing her a favor. Try this: "Girl, I feel bad because _____ obviously gets you really worked up. I want to be your sounding board, but I don't want you and I to both be stressed. How about we don't focus on that for a while so we can channel your energy into the amazing things you have going on, like _____."
2. Avoid the subject that really gets her going. It may seem obvious, but if there is one particular subject that really works her up, try your best not to bring it up. For chronic complainers, any topic is fair game. They can find a way to be miserable about anything. But the average person typically has a few particular sore spots.
3. Pivot gracefully. There is a gentle way to let her know she is being negative: by telling her you want the positive. Try this: "Well, tell me somethin' good! What's going *well* for you right now?"
4. Offer a solution. When women speak to each other, we spend more time questioning and commiserating than "solution" talk. While we do help each other solve problems, it often comes after first engaging in active listening and sympathetic chatter. This means it may stand out if, instead of offering a long period of standard commiserating, you cut to the chase by offering a solution. If she was looking for you to empathize with her one hundredth complaint, it may stop if she sees that you aren't willing to engage.
5. Refer her to someone who can help. When you friend begins to complain about the same thing she always complains about and you've already tried each of the strategies listed above, try something like this: "You've mentioned this to me a few times now but I don't think I can help you with it. Do you think at this point a professional can help you to stop feeling this way? I can help you look for someone if you want." Although you may be frustrated, I think it's best to deliver this option gently and earnestly, without sarcasm or exasperation. It's very possible that speaking with someone qualified to

help her won't just end the complaining, but address the root issue of her aggravation.

INHALING HER SMOKE

Since human beings are inherently social, our brains naturally and unconsciously mimic the moods of those around us, particularly people we spend a great deal of time with. This process is called *neuronal mirroring*, and it's the basis for our ability to feel empathy. The flip side, however, is that it makes complaining a lot like smoking — you don't have to do it yourself to suffer the ill effects.

You need to be cautious about spending time with people who complain about everything. Complainers want people to join their pity party so that they can feel better about themselves. Think of it this way: If a person were smoking, would you sit there all afternoon inhaling the second-hand smoke? You'd distance yourself, and you should do the same with complainers.

HOW TO STOP YOURSELF WHEN YOU'RE GUILTY

There are two things you can do when you feel the need to complain. One is to cultivate an attitude of gratitude. That is, when you feel like complaining, shift your attention to something that you're grateful for. Taking time to contemplate what you're grateful for isn't merely the right thing to do; it reduces the stress hormone cortisol by 23%. Research conducted at the University of California, Davis, found that people who worked daily to cultivate an attitude of gratitude experienced improved mood and energy and substantially less anxiety due to lower cortisol levels. Any time you experience negative or pessimistic thoughts, use this as a cue to shift gears and to think about something positive. In time, a positive attitude will become a way of life.

Think that's too good (and simple) to be true?

Dr. Rick Hanson, author of *Hardwiring Happiness*, explores the connection between happiness, habits, and neurology. He tells of a study he was involved with where several people were instructed to write something they're grateful for along with their reason why. (So for example, if you say you're grateful for your mother, you'd also write down that it's because she makes you feel loved and supported.) After 21 days of doing this, people who were testing as low-level pessimists were testing as low-level optimists. For those who had depression, the exercise helped with that as well.

The same study was also done with participants affected by chronic muscular disease, and after 6 months they were all able to reduce the amount of medication they were taking by 50%. The reason this worked is because it literally reprogrammed people's thinking. Dr. Hanson compares our brains to an "app" constantly running in the background. Instead of noticing all the things going wrong, your brain will be "scanning" for all the things going right in your world.

Y'all, this is no joke. This means despite what people tell us about how being a pessimist or optimist is out of our control, it turns out that we *do* have power over how we want to think.

Instead of viewing a negativity "call-out" as an offense, try to see it as a duty and a help. Tough-love friendship requires you to challenge and affirm your friends. Bringing your relationship into a space of light and positivity is you doing just that.

Holding Up Her Mirror

Tough-love friendship should be life-giving.

Unfortunately, the term "tough love" brings us images of brashness and insensitivity. But really, it's about doing hard things for the sake of the bigger picture.

Our friendships with other women require tough love because we need to do hard things not only to draw closer to each other, but for the sake of our individual growth.

In the survey I conducted earlier this year, one of the issues women said they deal with in their female friendships is body positivity. Many of us are vocal about our growing displeasure with our appearance and express that displeasure with our trusted friends. When a woman we love shares her struggles and dissatisfaction as it concerns her figure, we are charged with the responsibility to encourage her, showing her the beauty the world won't allow her to see.

Tough-love friendship should bring women to life. And I've noticed this is applicable most explicitly in the context of us recognizing our beauty.

According to the most recent survey conducted by Dove, 98% of women said there is something about their physical appearance they would change if they could. This isn't new information, but it puts evidence behind something we've always known to be true. Despite our "I am woman, hear me roar," most of us would alter something— however small and seemingly insignificant— about ourselves. I don't want to put shame behind that. We shouldn't feel bad about wanting to have certain parts of us look a certain way.

Until we get to a point of complete acceptance (which is an ongoing journey), there will always be moments where we wonder how we'd feel better about ourselves "if only."

IT'S HARD TO TREAT THE MIRROR

It's difficult to give a "tough-love call-out" on the issue of attractiveness and esteem because, as women, it is so tightly linked to our feelings of beauty and femininity. This is less about an intrinsic desire and more about feeling the weight of cultural reverence for aesthetics and unrealistic beauty standards.

This is natural. It is epidemic. It is likely simply a mark of a fundamental human desire— to be desirable, to be happy, and to be confident. Sadly, in a culture so obsessed with appearance, our desirability, happiness, and confidence have become inextricably linked to our appearance.

According to Scripture, we are God's handiwork (Ephesians 2:10). When He looks at women, He sees an absolute masterpiece. But it's so difficult to see ourselves through His eyes when we are exposed to thousands of images and messages a day that call us to question everything from our breasts to our skin and our hair.

When this is what we're up against, how do we "show up" for a friend who is unhappy with her appearance? How do we reaffirm a sister who can't see her beauty, and who suffers in her personal, professional, and or social life because of it?

While the average woman has one or two things she'd like to change, she is ultimately comfortable presenting herself to the world each day. But for some women, their anxiety and uncertainty, and self-dissatisfaction is utterly crippling, keeping them from hanging with friends, taking pictures, and even getting dressed. You can almost feel her discomfort, and it's hard to ignore is she's especially vocal about her physical insecurities.

But we struggle to be a tough love friend in these situations because it's a tender area for so many women; we don't know what to say, and oftentimes her insecurities mirror our own. How are we to address her dissatisfaction with her appearance when it hits too close to home? How are we supposed to look her in the eyes and remind her of her beauty when we still need someone to remind us of our own? How do we show up for her when we fear that our own shortcomings make us somehow less lovable and desirable?

I've found that, in speaking with women ages 16 to 55, this is a tricky issue to navigate because we're all trying to deal with it. Sure, many of us have days where no one can tell us *anything* because we look and feel So. Damn. Good. But there are other days when we see or hear something that triggers us into a spiral of doubt and self-consciousness.

Sometimes it's tough to have a friend who is dealing with physical esteem issues because her complaints about her face, body, skin, hair, and weight bring us down— and we feel guilty about it. It's so hard to listen to a woman we love pick herself apart because, depending on the frequency, that sadness and dejection are woefully contagious, and we find ourselves affected by her fretting.

What's worse is that we then feel guilty about feeling frustrated. We're supposed to be her friend, after all. We should know what to say to immediately lift her spirits, and we should be eager to walk with her during her periods of emotional unrest. We just … can't, and our *not knowing* it's the most complicated kind of response.

TELLING HABITS OF LOW PHYSICAL ESTEEM... AND WHAT TO AVOID

There are a few telling signs that your friend is struggling with physical insecurities.

Some of those signs include times when she:
- doesn't want to join group photos
- talks down about herself
- is nearly obsessive about her make-up, her hair being in place, etc
- makes self-deprecating jokes regarding her weight
- insults certain facial feature
- can't accept a guy being interested in her
- is constantly "fretting"

If you find that you simply don't know what to say or do when your friend comes down hard on herself, you're not alone. It's common to shy away or get a little awkward. Unequipped with a proper response can be more than unhelpful—it can exacerbate her low self-confidence. There are differences between how passive friendship and tough-love friendship address this issue.

Passive friendship changes the subject when a woman makes a negative remark about her appearance. This is dangerous because it makes her feel as though she wasn't heard, can confirm her insecurity that she's not enough when the comment isn't acknowledged, and can leave the implicit question hiding within her remarks unanswered.

Passive friendship also gives empty reassurances. It says, "Stop, you're beautiful!" It says "Oh my gosh, no you're perfect" and then changes the subject. It refuses to go to the heart of the matter.

Passive friendships operate outside of reality, telling her there's nothing wrong and everything is fine.

Impatient friendship uses shame to correct her behavior. "Jessica, you've got to stop saying stuff like that." "Come on, jump in the photograph! You're beautiful." putting her in positions she's not comfortable with for the sake of helping her "get over it."

Tough love invites. It does not passively shy away, nor does it unkindly force uncomfortable situations. It faces things head-on, with courage and compassion. Remember, tough love does not assume the role of a life coach or a therapist. You are not her pastor or her guidance counselor. You are her friend. And one of the most fundamental hallmarks of friendships is support. Sometimes real support comes in the form of a vulnerable, uncomfortable opportunity.

Showing tough love to a friend who is struggling with her appearance requires compassion, yet directness. It refuses to look away when she makes a self-deprecating joke about her weight. Instead, it calls for you to hold her hand, meet her eyes and really listen to her heart.

In fact, your courage in addressing her self-image can be the very thing that changes her perspective—and keeps her healthy.

In a 2014 study by Christine Logel, associate professor at the University of Waterloo, found that women who receive "acceptance messages" are more likely to either maintain their weight or weigh less over time. For women whose networks either criticized or failed to acknowledge their appearance, their weight increased over time. The study assessed college-aged women who felt dissatisfied with their weight. Over a period of 9 months they checked in with the women and found that those who had family and friends who told them they were fine maintained or lost weight. It turns out that saying encouraging our friends to accept themselves the way they are is good for them, but even suggesting they lose weight could have the opposite effect.

Tough love leads with vulnerability: "I gotta be honest: I never really know how to respond when you say things like that. I hate that we're all struggling to accept certain parts of ourselves— I know I am. And my hang-ups look different than yours. But I think you are beautiful, and I hope that's enough to get you to start believing it too."

There are variations of this message that you can deliver— you have to make it your own.

But the point is to address the very things that are real struggles for you. Are you uncomfortable when she hates on herself because you don't know how to respond? Tell her that. Does her obsession and self-deprecation send you into a spiral of your own? Say so.

No matter how stressful, true friendships demand that level of honesty. After hard truths are delivered, tough-love sticks around to work things out.

HOW TO SUPPORT YOUR FRIEND'S SELF-IMAGE

1. **Instead of ignoring her self-deprecating comments, lean in**. If she talks about how much she hates her lips, ask her why. There's a chance she's never spoken the reason aloud before. Walk with her through the reasons why she dislikes particular features and see if the conversation leads to other

issues that are the root of the problem. Is it because a guy she dated once commented on them? Is it because she's the only one in the family without a full pout? Sometimes just probing with questions can help her work out why she feels the way she does, which is the first step toward either changing the issue she's uncomfortable with or accepting it as is.

2. **Model a positive self-image**. There's no better way to help your friend see her own beauty than for you to first see your own. Resist the temptation to lament the parts of your appearance you don't like. Resist the urge to match her self-deprecation with your own. Since women have a higher level of agreeableness than men, it is normal for us to give a similar response to our friends' remarks as a show of sameness and solidarity. Recently, I made a complaint about my body to a close girlfriend. "Ugh, my thighs have seriously gotten so big! I mean, look at this," I said, jiggling my right leg with my fingertips. Her reaction totally gripped me: "Girl, I have big thighs too and you know what? It makes it easier to grip on to my husband in the bedroom!" We bot erupted in laughter, but she was right. And seeing the joy she took in her body's power made me view my legs differently.

3. **Hug her**. No, really. If she is heading down an especially dark spiral about how she looks, take the time to hug her. Among hundreds of recent studies examining the effects of this kind of touch, one finds that it can actually reduce anxiety in people with low self-esteem. Sander Koole who's a researcher at VU University in Amsterdam found that it can have a temporary calming effect on those who feel isolated. For your friend's particular complaints about feeling fatter, smaller, less attractive than everyone else, this can help her to feel connected and less alienated in her thoughts as she mentally separates herself from others in appearance.

4. **Help her to practice body neutrality.** This is a concept that has become popular over the past few years. It involves accepting that some days you'll love your body and some days you'll hate it (as opposed to body positivity, which encourages women to consistently remain in a state of loving their bodies). The movement of body neutrality also inspires women to focus less on their bodies' appearance and more on its abilities. For example, a new mom would be encouraged to stop obsessing over her body's new

stretch marks and, instead, to delight in the fact that it formed and birthed another human being.

But here is how my friends have affirmed me.

When I am drowning in a wave of self-criticism, I'm met with eye contact and words that remind me that my new shape is normal. Instead of blatant denials (What? Your weight hasn't changed a bit) or hollow encouragement ("You're beautiful! Stop!") they listen to me and meet my reality with an empathetic ear, and the "tough love friends" in my life have responded in the following ways:

- "Yeah, and I've got that too. I guess it happens after we have kids but I'm working on accepting this as my new shape. I mean, our bodies are f*cking powerful, right? That helps me not to get caught up in in the bullsh*t of fixating on how my stomach changed."
- "If you want, we can go to the gym in the mornings together and work on toning up."
- "Okay, so here's what I do: I started buying looser blouses and tucking them into my skirts. It still keeps me looking sexy after my stomach kind of got that "new mom" shape. Want me to show you the site where I got my new clothes?"

Every friendship is different, sure. But for me, it helped to have female friends who didn't deny my reality, who encouraged me to take action instead of letting me wallow, and who helped to shift my perspective when I was held captive to self-loathing. They reminded me of my beauty and potential.

We live in a distorted reality, and our Creator thinks we are masterpieces. We need our girls to hold a figurative (and sometimes literal) mirror to us and remind us of that. We need our friends to remind us when we've lost sight of the truth.

We need our friends to remind us when we are set back by a new scar, fluctuations in our weight, a belly stretched (or scarred) from pregnancy and delivery, new freckles or aging spots, and acne. We need women who say,

Yeah I see the blemishes. But you are so so beautiful, sister. And you are so much more than clumped mascara and numbers on a scale.

Tough love doesn't run for those uncomfortable moments. It sticks around and waits a while, because she needs us to hear her out… then bring her back to life.

One-Sided Friendships and Spiritual Perspective

Earlier this year I gathered 40 women and asked them about their number one "friendship issue". The top response: *I feel like my friendship is one-sided.*

I've heard this sentiment echoed in various arenas: Both in my teaching days and now in my coaching days, women often express to me their growing frustration surrounding feelings of imbalance in their friendships. Believing themselves to be the *giver*, they express feelings of being used and overlooked. This leads to questions about the other woman's commitment to the friendship or their generosity being taken advantage of. Some are ready to give up on the friendship altogether.

WHY IT FEELS OFF-BALANCE

While it's difficult to address the topic of feeling used, it's necessary. And while the very thought of telling your girl that you feel taken advantage of can send chills of anxiety up your spine, there's a way to tackle it.

When you begin to wonder if you're the one "doing all the work," consider three possible reasons you may feel that way:

1. Your girl sees friendships as transactional.

When some people attach to others, it is because they are looking to fulfill certain needs. Whether they want someone to hang out with on Saturday nights, listen to their troubles, or rescue them from their problems, "friendship" is merely a title that they extend to people they can benefit from. This doesn't make them malicious— in fact, many are unaware they're operating from such a selfish place. But when dealing with someone who is looking for emotional, physical, mental, or financial support from their friends— without concern for what they themselves can contribute to a close, mutually beneficial relationship— it doesn't take long for the woman being used to begin feeling the weight of the expectation. This is not a gender-exclusive flaw. It is merely a fact of humankind. Because of our various upbringings and the lessons we learned about relationships, we enter into friendships with varying standards and criteria.

2. You and your friend have different expectations of what is required.

It is quite possible that, if you are feeling like you are doing most of the giving in a friendship, you have different ideas and opinions of friendship than the women you're involved with. If friendship to you involves talking on the phone and listening to each other's issues, but for another it means hanging out occasionally and tagging each other in memes on Instagram, disappointment is inevitable. The larger picture is two women who have different ideas of the demands of their relationship, which often come to a head when one feels slighted, misused, or underserved by the other. The smaller picture is that the two women have different ideas that can be reconciled if only they had a conversation sharing their respective needs, desires, and boundaries.

3. You're not as close as you think you are.

Sociologist Charles Cooley suggested that there are two groups that we all belong to: primary and secondary. Primary groups are networks of people we trust who give us love and support. There is a familiarity and expectation of mutual caring. In a secondary group, however, we exchange little personal information and there aren't strong emotional ties.

I believe that the reason for some of our discrepancies in our expectations is because we are engaged in relationships with women whose "primary group" we're not a part of. Though it hurts to realize, there are times when we feel connected to a woman and therefore (unintentionally) place expectations on her, but she does not reciprocate because she doesn't view the friendship with the same priority.

4. You define friendship differently.

Is it possible that your friend is in a space where she only has time for texts and the occasional hangout? Is she looking for convenient dialogue and a good laugh while you're seeking weekly chats and emotional support? There's a chance that you're in different seasons, which in turn demand different capacities for engagement and support. If that's the case, you have to evaluate whether you have the ability (and willingness) to step back and meet your friend where she is, or if you're looking for someone who can match and mirror your effort.

STEWING ON THE IMBALANCE

I went to a party last year and found myself (as always) suddenly surrounded by a group of women in the kitchen (why do we congregate there?). I noticed them speaking in hushed voices, careful not to be heard by someone particular, it seemed. When I asked what was going on, one of the ladies spoke up.

"It's Jackie. I love her, don't get me wrong. But whenever we're all talking about something, like our jobs or boyfriends or other personal stuff or whatever, she just listens. That's it. She'll listen to everyone else talk but she never ever shares herself. I only recently realized that and I'm starting to feel like it's seems so one-sided."

I went into coach mode, encouraging her to examine alternative perspectives.

"That's frustrating. You're investing in her, emotionally, but she's not giving it back to you." I worked to validate her feelings before prompting her to entertain a new angle to the narrative she'd written.

"I mean, yeah. Like, what is that?" she seemed more perplexed than upset.

I asked, "I wonder if she's doing it intentionally or if that's just how she is. Have you ever mentioned it to her?"

"No, but I mean, do I really need to tell someone 'We should be sharing equally'? That's just what friends do."

Asha was frustrated because her expectation is that a friend shares as much with her because she's committed to doing the same— as mutual friends should. But she hadn't considered that perhaps Jackie *did* think she was sharing, yet kept a guard up due to experiences we weren't aware of. It's possible that Jackie is simply a great listener, overly cautious about making the situation about herself and determined to listen more than she speaks. It's possible that there are things she wants to open up about but doesn't yet feel comfortable. It's possible that Jackie was behaving according to cultural norms. And it's also possible that Asha is more invested in the friendship than Jackie— which happens.

Either way, without lovingly addressing it head on, each girl would continue to develop her own limited narrative which inevitably creates confusion, misunderstanding, and possibly resentment; it would certainly create emotional distance as Asha shares less and they gradually spend less time together because of it.

Their expectations of the friendship were not equal. But how is Jackie to know Asha's disappointment? How is Jackie to understand the attention and reciprocity her friend needs to feel close? How can Asha exercise an attitude of curiosity instead of accusation? What might be revealed if Asha invited her into a dialogue using vulnerability, telling Jackie that she wants to feel closer but it's hard when she feels she knows so little?

BENEFITS OF CALLING IT OUT

Tough-love friendship is required when one woman begins feeling like the relationship is one-sided. Remember, this kind of friendship benefits the initiator, the receiver, and the overall bond.

THE INITIATOR BENEFITS: For the woman who feels that she is more invested in the friendship, she must call-out the situation because she will either grow resentful or eventually burnout from working to maintain a friendship that demands but does not provide. She may also find, in initiating a conversation about how she feels, that she *is* giving too much, either as a people-pleaser or one eager for connection and companionship, and will therefore be able to begin shifting both her behavior and expectations. After a conversation about the expectations within the friendship, tough love is courageous enough to objectively assess all that was brought to the table and walk away if there is no willingness to equally share the joys, hardships and effort of a healthy friendship.

Remember to apply the S.E.T the M.I.C Framework before inviting her into a conversation about feeling like you're putting in more effort.

THE RECEIVER BENEFITS: For the woman who is taking more than she is giving in a relationship, confrontation is necessary for her to see that she A. is wrong for being a user and needs to stop (if her "transactional" mentality is intentional) or B. has needs, habits, and desires that make her friend feel used (if unintentional). Either way, tough love friendship allows the one doing the "taking" an opportunity to rectify what's taking place, which most times is completely innocent.

THE OVERALL FRIENDSHIP BENEFITS: As soon as one woman begins to feel like she is doing more of the emotional, mental, or financial labor, it becomes a threat to the overall health and intimacy of their friendship. Closeness can not be achieved when one secretly wonders if her friendship is appreciated or if it's being taken for granted. With that kind of suspicion present, emotional distance becomes inevitable.

Tough love friendship doesn't passively harbor suspicions (*Does she only need me because I am the only one who listens to her drama? Does she only hang around because I pay for our outings? Does she expect that I'll always be the one to initiate hangouts? Am I more invested than she is?*). It does the hard work of calling out the imbalance with compassion and directness, and it welcomes dialogue about each woman's expectations and experiences, ultimately enriching the friendship and allowing each woman to operate in confidence, informed of her friends' needs.

APPLYING A SPIRITUAL PERSPECTIVE

As I spent time speaking with women about their friendships, this theme of one-sidedness has emerged consistently as the number one conflict in their friendships. It also seems to be the issue we are most uncomfortable to confront.

I believe that as much as we can equip ourselves with tactical strategies and inspiring messages about tough-love friendships, it helps to apply a spiritual perspective as well. This way, we zoom out of the situation and examine our situation from a lens that tells us what the Bible has to say about conflict in our friendships.

To explore this idea further, I interviewed Blake Giuchet, host of *The Crappy Christian Podcast*. I've been listening to her show since it began, and I knew she'd be the perfect woman to offer insights on what God has to say about how to approach hard conversations.

Here are a few of the clips from that conversation, along with Bible points to reference for you to dive deeper.

Q: How does the Bible offer practical and loving advice for how to handle tough items in our friendships? How do you interpret its message for confronting a friend?

As far as confronting a friend who's in a season of self-destruction or who has hurt or wronged you, it's Matthew 18. It literally walks out how to Biblically engage in conflict. The passage says that if your brother sins against you, you go and have a conversation with them. Jesus is giving us, word-for-word, a way to resolve it: Go and talk to your friend, it says. If he listens, the sin is done, it's forgiven, it's forgotten and you move forward. If your brother won't listen to you, then bring two or three together and then approach them, and if they still won't listen then go to the elders.

God knew that conflict would be a part of our lives. God knew that conflict would be a part of our friendships, so he gave us this perfect step-by-step outline ... but yes, it's still really difficult to walk out.

[Blake is referring here to the book of Matthew chapter 18 verse 15.]

Q: How does motive play a role in confronting a friend about hard things?

A: If I'm coming to you in humility and grace, then I don't have anything to fear.

ONE-SIDED FRIENDSHIPS AND SPIRITUAL PERSPECTIVE

It doesn't mean I won't be nervous or a little scared, but that's where it's all about motive. The Bible talks about that. Wherever the word "pride" appears in the Bible, it's often adjacent to the word "fool". Pride is foolishness and it leads to foolishness, so if you're engaged in conflict or difficult conversations and you're only out to say "My feelings are hurt and I want you to apologize", no good is gonna come from that. But if you approach it with a spirit of love and kindness and the person still has a bad reaction, it will be hard and sad and exhausting, but you'll be able to walk through it knowing you did your best.

[For reference: 1 Corinthians 4:14; Ephesians 4:15]

Q: The Bible speaks a lot to peace and wisdom. What applications do you find for the Bible's definitions of those words and how we can go about achieving them in our friendships?

If you know your motives and your heart and you came up to the plate with everyone's best intention in mind, yes it will hurt and will likely be another matter of forgiveness. But it's okay to feel okay afterwards too. You might feel like "I feel like I should be wrecked by this," but you'll have peace and assurance— at least that's what happened with me recently, during a hard conversation with a friend— because I was walking in who God made me. I mean, if you listen to the podcast, you know that I'm an enneagram 8, which means hard words come easily to me, and I have way more experience on that end of the spectrum—ripping someone apart and then feeling convicted.

Just in the day-to-day friendship... you have to be able to say the hard things. Truth in love. Over and over in the Psalms and Proverbs and in the New Testament Scripture talks about being of wise counsel and being a wise friend and surrounding yourself with wise people. Wise doesn't mean be a pushover. It doesn't mean tell people what they want to hear. Wisdom is all-encompassing which means it includes saying the hard things. I'm definitely in a season of working to surround myself with women who are wise and will use that wisdom for my benefit....And vice versa. It means we can look into each other's lives and ask

Do you really need to do that? Do you really need to say that? Could you be doing this better? Was that fair?

Now, you don't want all of your conversations to look like that. It's supposed to be fun and life-giving and enjoyable. But in the moment when the Spirit leads you and prompts you, wisdom is about having those conversations and feeling safe to do so. We can foster that environment by being accepting and receptive and taking down our walls and not being defensive—which is hard for me! But I'm getting there.

[For reference: Proverbs 13:20; Proverbs 27:17]

There is much to be said about applying a spiritual perspective to friendship. When dealing with two varying viewpoints, egos, and experiences, it often helps to assume a more aerial view and think of the relationship from a more holistic space. Remembering the purpose of companionship and conflict can re-frame the way we approach difficult sues with the women we love most.

A FINAL CALL TO ACTION

We can have the meaningful friendships that we're after. If we're willing to identify our personal insecurities, examine culture's influence on our behavior, and put in the actual work that's required, we can enjoy the fullness of relationships with other women.

As study after study continues to show the impact of our social health on our physical and emotional well-being, there's simply too much at stake. Let's break the unspoken "girl code" of accepting drama and miscommunication as staples of female friendship. Let's work together to boldly address the awkward subjects we often deal with alone, feeling frustrated and disappointed when another friendship falls short of our expectations.

It doesn't have to be that way.

Tough-love friendship is for women who want relationships that allow them to share themselves fully, affirm others openly, preserve boundaries firmly, and challenge others gracefully. Once we begin putting this into practice, we'll be well on our way toward more meaningful friendships that stand the test of time.

We just have to stir up the courage and put in the work.

Discussion Questions

Chapter 1

1. The author begins the chapter with a specific time when she went without tough-love in her friendships. Can you recall a particular time when you failed to give or receive tough-love? How does that particular experience affect how you view "tough-love friendships" now?
2. In what context do you normally hear the phrase "tough love" being used? How does that affect how you feel about "tough love" in the context of friendship?

Chapter 2

1. Danielle outlines the four "courage sectors" of the Tough-Love Friendship Model: *Sharing, Preserving, Affirming,* and *Challenging.* Which is the easiest for you to practice? Which is the most difficult?

Chapter 3

1. Review the chapter's description of the various attachment types. Which best describes you and how might it be (positively or negatively) affecting your relationships with other women?
2. Consider the following attitudes:

I'll never be as close to new friends as I was with my old friends... If a friend offends or betrays me, I'll just replace her... If I don't hit it off with a new girl, I have to let it go... Real friendship shouldn't require effort.

DISCUSSION QUESTIONS

Have you ever adopted any of these attitudes? If so, how did it affect your ability to draw close to/ experience intimacy with other women?

Chapter 4

1. The author explores the idea of "cut-off culture" as a consequence of our inability to have tough conversations. Do you agree or disagree with this?

Chapter 5

1. This chapter lists several examples of gender bias along with ways each might affect female friendships. Can you think of other (positive or negative) stereotypes and the impact they may have on how we deal with other women?
2. Has a desire to be "liked" ever kept you from freely speaking your mind?

Chapter 6

1. This chapter explores the ways our need to belong drives our friendships. How well do you monitor your feelings of loneliness and its impact on the relationships you've formed?

Chapter 7

1. When confronting a friend about a sensitive topic, women can either be overly concerned with her emotions (and therefore reluctant to have the conversation) or unaffected by the other's emotions (and therefore come across as harsh). Where do you fall on that spectrum?

Chapter 8

1. Consider the negative consequences of holding your true feelings inside.

What impact can this have on the person withholding their truth? What impact can the silence have on the friendship itself?

Chapter 9

1. The author provides a framework to use when approaching a friend with a hard subject. Which parts of the SET the MIC framework pose the most difficulty for you?

Chapter 10

1. Danielle lists the various "Tough-Love Response Types". Which describes you?
2. Dani Pascarella suggests accepting negative feedback systematically, listing specific ways she works to process criticism. Have you ever considered taking this kind of approach in your personal relationships? Do you think a systematic process would be helpful or hurtful outside of the professional realm?

Chapter 11

1. How do you define *judgment*? does it ever have a place in friendship? Explain.

Chapter 12

1. In this chapter, Danielle encourages readers to identify and examine their personal insecurities and the ways in which they impacted their relationships with others. Look at the four sectors of the Tough-Love Friendship Model. Do personal insecurities affect your ability to exercise any of the sectors?

Chapter 13

DISCUSSION QUESTIONS

1. This chapter explores gossip and complaining in in female friendships. Do you think a little bit of each is healthy in a friendship, or do you believe its best to have a "zero-tolerance policy"?
2. Has anyone ever confronted you about the issue of gossip or negativity? If so how did you take it? If not, how do you think you would take it?

Chapter 14

1. How well do you monitor the ways in which social media affects your personal body image?
2. The author examines the ways our responses to a friend's self-deprecation can be helpful or harmful. How do you typically respond to a friend who "hates on" herself? Why do you take that approach?

Chapter 15

1. According to the survey Danielle conducted in early 2019, the number one complaint women had in their friendships is feeling that they're one-sided. Have you ever felt this way? What do you think was the reason for the imbalance?
2. How does applying a spiritual perspective to the worldly experience of conflict illuminate any of your current situations?
3. *Give it a Rest* ends with a call to action. As you finished the book, what is the first step you feel most compelled to take on your journey toward creating more meaningful friendships?

Acknowledgements

What a journey.

I'd like to thank every single woman who shared her story with me to make this book possible. The interviews required you to be vulnerable. I respect your courage and appreciate your insight.

To friends and family who let me bounce ideas off of them, please know how deeply grateful I am for your patience and your time.

To the members of the GIVE IT A REST Movement, thank you! If you are attending events, booking coaching sessions, and reading the articles, you were a part of this journey. I'm so glad we're in this together.

I'd also like to thank my mother, Merrie Allen Allmon, for showing me what commitment and discipline look like. Mom, after watching you write two books of your own (both after the age of 50!), I was inspired to give finally give voice to my own. Thank you for demonstrating how to be patient with the process.

Finally, I'd like to extend my greatest thanks to my husband, Ryan. You were my rock throughout this entire project. Thank you for letting me spend evenings at random coffee shops to write and research. Thank you for trusting me when I said, "It will be worth it, I promise!" And thank you for watching the baby when I needed "just one more hour". I couldn't have produced *Give it a Rest* without your support. I love you.

About the Author

Danielle Bayard Jackson is a certified women's coach specializing in friendship and communication. She is also the founder of GIVE IT A REST Movement, an education and event hub for Millennial women to receive personal coaching as they work to navigate social relationships. As a publicist, educator, and coach, Danielle has spent the last ten years of her career teaching, observing, and interviewing women ages 16-55. She uses her studies as a member of the American Sociological Association to encourage women to form and nurture honest relationships.

Danielle is also the co-founder of STRIDE Media group— a boutique public relations agency working to "give women the shine they deserve" by pairing female and minority clients with journalists who will share their stories with diverse audiences.

A busy "mompreneur", Danielle lives in Florida with her husband Ryan and son Elijah.

Give it a Rest is her first book.

You can connect with me on:

- https://www.giveitarestmovement.com
- https://www.facebook.com/giveitarestmovement

Made in the USA
Middletown, DE
15 May 2021